Learning Golf
with Manuel

by John Hayes

Learning Golf with Manuel
By John A. Hayes
c. 2009

Published by Hayes Golf Pro Publishing
523 Fairways Circle
St. Louis, MO 63141 (www.learninggolfwithmanuel.com)
email: jh@learninggolfwithmanuel.com

Printed in the United States of America

ISBN: 978-0-615-23134-1
Library of Congress Number Pending
Price: $18.00

Hayes, John A., 1957 –
Learning Golf with Manuel

ISBN:
1. Golf. 2. Golf techniques. 3. Golf biography.

Dedication

This book can only be dedicated to Manuel de la Torre. Here are just a few highlights from his 60+ year career in golf:

Manuel finished second in the
1942 National Intercollegiate Championship.

He graduated from Northwestern University in
1947 with a degree in Business Administration.

He finished in 3rd place at the Tucson Open in 1950 and
2nd place at the Lakewood Open in 1951 on the PGA Tour.

He was named the Head Golf Professional at
Milwaukee Country Club in 1951.

He was a five-time Wisconsin State Open Champion.

He won the 1973 National Open Seniors Classic.

He tied for 1st place in the National PGA Senior
Championship in 1978 and lost in a playoff.

He was the very first recipient of the National PGA
Teacher of the Year Award in 1986.

He was inducted into the World Golf
Teachers Hall of Fame in 2005.

He was inducted into the PGA of
America Hall of Fame in 2006.

Acknowledgments

T he primary contributor to this book is Manuel de la Torre. He has given all of the lessons and spent all of the hours thinking of the different ways for his students to play better golf. He has also spent countless hours sharing his time with anyone who has a desire to become a golf professional and instructor. Fortunately this has multiplied his positive influence many times on the golf world. The people of Milwaukee Country Club should be thanked for sharing their professional and giving him a home since 1951. Manuel spent many hours with me going through every lesson in this book to be sure that the wording is as clear as it can be and he continues to be a real gift to all of the golfers that he sees. I regret that I can only give a small glimpse of what Manuel brings to every student who walks down the path to take a lesson.

I must acknowledge all of golf students/friends and the golf communities that I have worked with: Forest Hills Country Club, Bellerive Country Club and Normandie Golf Course, all of which are in St. Louis, Missouri. The thousands of golf lessons that I have given and the many relationships that I have developed have made all of the difference for me.

Finally, I thank Brian Hayes, my brother, and Mary Hayes, my wife, for the kind and necessary proofreading on this project.

– John Hayes

Foreword
by Martha Nause

T here are few times in our lives when we have the opportunity to work with and learn from a true master. I've had that opportunity as an LPGA touring professional; Manuel de la Torre is that master. Upon graduation from college, I decided to embark upon the adventure of playing professional golf. I was lucky to book two thirty-minute lessons with Manuel the summer prior to getting on the tour. I had taken golf lessons many other times, but after those two half hour lessons, I was never more energized and excited in my life. The golf swing, as presented to me by Manuel, made so much sense. The questions he asked me during those lessons were tough ones as I'd never really thought about the swing prior to that. When I didn't know the answer to his questions, he asked more questions until I finally arrived at the answer he was looking for. Then and only then did I start to understand the swing upon which I would build my career. Now, thirty years later I reflect back on those two lessons as the beginning of my adventure – not so much the playing of professional golf but, rather, the learning of the nuances of the game and the swing, and teaching the golf swing that I have learned from one of the masters of our sport.

Lessons with Manuel are amazing experiences. Unlike so many other lessons I've taken in my life, I've never been challenged to think and to understand the why of what was being taught as I am, to this day, with Manuel. Manuel wants his students to understand the golf swing as a simple concept, but he also knows that though the concept is simple, the execution of it may not be. From that first day on Manuel's lesson tee, I saw the beauty of the swing concept he was teaching. It made so much sense; could it really be that simple? And if it made so much sense, how could I not embrace it? Manuel relates the golf swing to many other things we do in life: performing other sporting motions, driving a car, drawing a picture, as well as using our minds prior to any action we take. That is the beauty of Manuel's concept of the golf swing as well as the genius of his teaching. Manuel's brilliance as a teacher doesn't stop with only the motion of swinging the golf club. His insistence on his students using their minds properly has always been important in his teaching as well. Sports psychologists have been utilized in golf instruction for the past twenty years or so. Manuel talked about using your mind properly well before that.

After retiring from a twenty-two year career of golf on the LPGA tour, I've taken Manuel's concept of playing golf and swinging the golf club to the lesson tee as I now teach and coach, passing along the knowledge I've accumulated from him through all these years. I've found that Manuel's swing concept holds up across the board, from beginners to advanced players. I now consult with Manuel as much on how to teach as I do on how to actually swing the golf club.

In the book *Learning Golf with Manuel*, John Hayes gives the readers a glimpse into how remarkable Manuel is as both a teacher of the golf swing and as a person. Each chapter captures the essence of not only what Manuel teaches but also his innate ability to connect the golf swing to other common everyday things we do in life. He is truly a man who loves teaching the golf swing. As a student of Manuel's, you always have his undivided attention. There is nothing more important to Manuel during a lesson than his student, and he wants that student to understand what is being taught. People have told me that they think taking a lesson from Manuel can be intimidating. Looking at him physically, intimidation would probably be the farthest thing from a person's mind. Manuel is patient yet persistent, asking many questions to help his students understand. His persistence and his questions allow the students to find the answers, making his teaching style a challenging yet wonderful learning ground.

As a teacher using Manuel's swing concept and teaching style, I found John Hayes' book, *Learning Golf with Manuel*, to be a great resource and complement to Manuel's own book about the golf swing. John has captured not only the content of what Manuel teaches but has accurately recorded conversations Manuel is likely to have with a student during a lesson. As someone who has taken lessons from Manuel for thirty years, so many of the chapters brought me right back to the teaching tee at Milwaukee Country Club and the times I've worked with him since 1977.

Manuel de la Torre is a humble man who has devoted his life to teaching the golf swing, and I am so fortunate to be a student of his. I've had golf lessons with Manuel over the phone, in the rain, in the snow, early in the morning and late at night. Manuel loves giving golf lessons and talking about the golf swing! I've heard Manuel say to people who tell him he could charge $1000 per person for a lesson instead of his customary $40, "I'd rather give one thousand people a lesson for $1.00, than one person a lesson for $1000.00!" That is the answer of a true master.

Martha Nause

Head Coach, Macalester College Men's and Women's golf teams.
Three LPGA tour victories from 1978 – 1999, with one major.
Over $1,300,000 in career earnings.
Qualified for the U.S. Women's Open in 2008.

Introduction

(I) have spent more than 100 days of my life watching and listening to Manuel de la Torre teach golf. Most of these days began by 8:30 a.m. and continued through a dinner at night where Manuel was still answering questions about the lessons of that day. This experience began for me on September 26, 1983, and I wrote a page of notes about the lesson I received from Manuel that day. At the end of the day of lessons, I showed Manuel this written summary of his lesson with me. He read through it and stopped at the third point where he took my pencil and crossed out one word. The sentence read: "Simply swing the club forward with the arms (the upper arms) from the top of the swing through to the finish in one, uninterrupted motion." He had crossed out the word "through," and he asked me, "Through what?" He had spent a good portion of the lesson with me on removing the tension and effort that I exerted to try to hit the ball hard and far, but with one word I tried to sneak it all back in. I have that sheet of paper framed, and while Manuel did a good job of crossing out that one word, I know that I still put it back in on too many swings.

Manuel's concept of what the student needs to do to produce good shots is very simple. It is all laid out by the ninth page in Manuel's book, *Understanding the Golf Swing*. The concept has not changed in all of these years, but the subtle explanations, the everyday life examples, the innovative ways that Manuel has to get the student to perform in a better way are still being developed in every lesson that is given.

My intent in writing this book is to give a glimpse of what it is like to take a golf lesson with Manuel. This text is the result of many years of note-taking that took place on the practice tee, and I tried to keep the feel of that situation where the student is asked questions, ponders the answers, changes intentions, is given explanations, reaches new understandings, and generally produces better swings. All of this in a brief space of time. During a lesson, Manuel will ask the student to use his or her mind to try to become associated with the perfection that is a swinging motion. Manuel will often have more belief in and respect for the abilities of the students than they have in themselves. This will usually change by the end of the lesson as the student understands and knows that he or she can really do it.

While respected by many of the noted teachers of today, Manuel is sometimes considered an "old-timer" who is good with beginners, but not quite modern and up-to-date with his teaching. I have enjoyed seeing and learning from many of the most highly-regarded teachers in golf over the years, and I can say that Manuel is the most sophisticated and coherent golf teacher that I have ever seen. He is not a self-promoter and is always more concerned about the student than his own reputation.

I have had great concern in writing this book, because those that know Manuel realize how important he considers every word in an explanation of the golf swing. Please know that all of the good parts are just accurate representations of what Manuel has said and done during the golf lessons, and the awkward phrases are all mine. I am proud that I spent several hours with Manuel at Milwaukee Country Club and elsewhere going over every lesson/section in this book to get it correct, in addition to multiple phone conversations. Besides being a great teacher, he is the best proofreader that you will find. The format of the book is simply to have a quote from Manuel followed by an explanation of the circumstances in a lesson or teaching seminar that led to his comment.

Manuel's excellence as a teacher is not just the completeness and the correctness of his concept: it is the idea that the students are given something that, the more they do it, the better they will become. The student is not given a half-truth, or some golf instruction cliché that can be overdone and will create problems down the road. Also, the student will leave the lesson saying, "I understand this and I can do this. It works! I can't wait to go play." Manuel explains the physics and the geometry, but it is his understanding of the psychology that makes the lesson such a beneficial experience for his students.

John Hayes
November 2008

Note from the Author

If you would like to use these stories as a more tradition-
al golf instruction book, then I would advise reading
the following stories in the sequence listed: grip - #58
and #98; the address position - #15; the swing - #18, #19, #31,
#59, #27 and #30; response to the swing - #91 and #35; mental
aspects - #1, #75 and #54; putting - #82, #83 and #9.

A brand new golfer could read the stories on the grip, #58
and #98, and then try a sequence that I saw Manuel use with a
golfer who had never played before. After helping the student
place her hands on the club, Manuel asked the student to set the
clubhead on the grass next to the golf ball in the address position. Next he asked the student to set the club on her right
shoulder (for a right-handed golfer). [The student may need to
be told to do this in the "golf direction," meaning backward and
not directly in front of him or her as if to chop wood.] Then the
student was asked to set the clubhead back on the grass next to
the ball, the same as it was at the address position. Then the student was asked to set the clubhead on the grass on the target-
side of the ball, and from there the student was asked to set the
club on the left shoulder and to allow the right heel to come up
in response to this movement. The student was asked to repeat
this sequence a few times: the clubhead on the grass, club on
the right shoulder, clubhead back on the grass behind the ball,
clubhead on the grass on the target-side of the ball, and club on
the left shoulder.

Now the student was asked to alter this sequence by putting
the club OVER the right shoulder rather than setting it on the
right shoulder. From the address position the student was asked
to put the club over the right shoulder, then put the clubhead
back on the grass, then put the clubhead on the grass on the target-side of the ball, and then put the club OVER the left shoulder as the right heel is allowed to come up in response to the
movement. This sequence was repeated a few times, and then it
was altered again where the golfer did not stop at the positions
but simply allowed the club to pass through the positions.

During this sequence the ball was removed, and the student was asked to "brush the grass" in the ball area on the way to going over the left shoulder at the finish of the forward swing. This sequence was repeated a few times. Finally, Manuel asked the student to go through the last sequence with the golf ball on the grass, but he emphasized that there should be no special concern for hitting the golf ball, but to be sure to get the clubhead back on the grass during the forward swing. I can't tell you that every shot that she hit was perfect, but she produced many nice shots and was looking like a golfer in less than 30 minutes. Most importantly, this student now had the belief that she was capable of producing the motion needed to propel the golf ball. The new golfer should also read story #76.

Contents
Manuel de la Torre Quotes

14. "Don't leave here saying, 'de la Torre says the body doesn't move.' "

15. "Don't leave here saying, 'de la Torre wants the ball in the center.' "

16. "My Dad never asked what I shot."

17. "The wrists hinge on the plane."

18. "I don't care about the length of the backswing as long as the hands are quiet."

19. "In a platoon of marching soldiers, who moves first? Who leads?"

20. "Does an infielder in baseball take a step backward before throwing the ball?"

21. "What was the President's name in 1952?"

22. "Throw a baseball overhand, and now throw a baseball sidearm. Does the body move differently for each throw?"

23. "Where is the muscle memory?"

24. "Why do we take a divot? Because the knees increase the flex in response to the forward swing."

25. "The shoulders **start** with, **stay** with, and **stop** with the clubhead in the backswing."

26. "Using the arms does not mean you use muscular strain."

27. "If you **USE** your arms, you are not **USING** your shoulders."

28. "I very seldom change the speed of a person's back-swing."

29. "Why does the right arm supply more of the speed on the forward swing?"

30. "When I want to send the ball farther, I don't think of clubhead speed. I concern myself with arm speed."

31. "The hands simply hold it. The arms swing it."

32. "When your arms stop, the clubhead cannot get very far out there (toward the target)."

33. "In the backswing I use my hands. I don't get involved with where my wrists hinge."

34. "The moment you anticipate the return to the ball, you cut off the backswing."

35. "In any swing where the club reaches the horizontal level past the ball, the back foot should be straight up."

36. "Let the club go to zero (m.p.h.) in the backswing."

37. "The hand level will change at the top of the backswing from club to club because of the different planes of the swings."

38. "I don't get too involved with saying, 'Use the hands in the backswing,' because there is only one way to get it over the shoulder."

39. "Even if I wanted to quadruple the arm speed on the forward swing, the backswing (speed) would stay the same."

40. "Once you set the **direction** on the backswing, keep going in that same direction."

41. "If you want to make the backswing longer, then **everything** goes back farther."

42. "I prefer to have the player keep the weight equal (50% left and 50% right) than to try to stay centered."

43. "If the plane of the film that is used to photograph the swing is parallel to the actual plane of the swing, you can see the shape of the swing."

44. "How can the right hip move if the right knee doesn't move?"

45. "In the forward swing, the center goes down a little, but not forward until after impact."

46. "I would rather see a reverse-pivot, than moving off the ball (to the right) in the backswing."

47. "Why are the hips turned toward the target ("open") at impact? Because the body uncoils from the bottom up."

48. "Don't force the right foot up. Let it go. Your right leg should be very relaxed."

49. "If you keep your right knee flexed, you restrict your turn."

50. "Does the right elbow get closer to the right hip during the forward swing? No it doesn't."

51. "When you add knee bend (at address), the body moves away from the ball in order to regain balance."

52. "Your shoulders rotate at right angles to your spine. I rotate around my center, the midpoint between the shoulders."

53. "I don't like the word *release*. If you release a prisoner, it means you held him back for a while."

54. "My concept has never missed a shot. I have missed plenty of shots."

55. "If you have a tough customer, you should see how happy you can make him rather than trying NOT to make him angry."

56. "After you hole your last putt on the 18th green, you must wait until the next day to hit your next shot."

57. "In putting your legs can stay motionless."

58. "With 4 or 5-year-old juniors, I would start them with a 10-finger grip. With 8 to 10-year-old juniors, I would start them with an overlapping grip."

59. "It's all the same thing; you are trying to take the ball-hitting attitude out of there."

60. "What is on the plane? The swing is on the plane."

61. "Wrist action is essential. Hand action is terrible."

62. "Why do I repeat, over and over, what I want them to do? Is it because they are not smart enough? No! It is because I don't want their mind to wander."

63. "They tell you today that your hands should be ahead of the ball at impact. That, to me, is a ridiculous thing."

64. "Now, very slowly, push my club back."

65. "Don't ever tell anyone that they don't hit the ball far enough."

66. "Is the **POSITION** of the club toe-up and parallel (to the target line) important? Not to me. The **MOTION** that gets it there is important.

67. "I don't practice the driver very much."

68. "I disagree with using the video to show people what is wrong. I don't care about what I do wrong."

69. "If the right heel doesn't respond, it forces you to move from up here (the shoulders)."

70. "If you are hitting a small shot to the target, your mind will control the size and the speed, but **YOU** control the direction."

71. "Don't try to swing it to parallel (to the target line) past the ball, or you will pull the shot to the left."

72. "We should be slow instructors, but effective."

73. "Swing at that spot, and the spot is on the circle."

74. "When do you feel that the sweet spot of the clubhead has met the ball?"

75. "You can only have one thought at a time, so if you think of all of the different parts, then your mind is jumping around-that makes your muscles jump around."

76. "There are two things that beginners want to do: 1) get the ball up in the air and 2) hit it far. You have to eliminate those things."

77. "With muscular tension, the first thing that goes is distance. The second thing that goes is direction."

78. "The best explanation is that, it is the compression of the sand against the ball that gets it out of the bunker."

79. "Why do I say **SCRAPE** the sand rather than **HIT** the sand?"

80. "There are three different ways to play a fairway bunker shot."

81. "On little shots, I don't like this idea of accelerating through the ball."

82. "I visualize the ball rolling on the line while I make the (putting) stroke. I don't get involved with the mechanics."

83. "Some people putt in reverse. They use their arms going back and their hands going forward."

84. "What should you try to do on an approach shot?"

85. "Your intent needs to change from here [the ball] to out there [the target].

86. "You have to watch when you make a change with a player."

87. "I want to remember the good things because I can build on the good things. I can't build on the bad things."

88. "You don't beat them with your distance. Beat them with your game."

89. "Big divots are caused by two things: 1) the desire to hit down and 2) using the hands on the forward swing."

90. "Nothing goes from the top [end of the backswing] until the arms set everything in motion."

91. "The arms initiate the swinging of the club. The feet initiate the body response."

92. "Either you are ball-oriented, or you are not. It is just that simple."

93. Question: How can the correct use of the arms feel so effortless? Manuel: "It is just like throwing a ball."

94. "Remembering the color of the flag will do you no good. Do you remember the **LOCATION** of the flag?"

95. "My mental shot has no distance or elevation."

96. "I don't want to make a slicer hook the ball."

97. "The quickest way to work on balance is to hold the finish."

98. "I don't look at the knuckles on a player's grip. Why not?"

99. "When you squeeze the hands, they should not change position."

100. "Why does the head move backward during the forward swing?"

101. "Where is the target in relation to you?"

102. "The **DIRECTION** of the backswing and the forward swing should be the same, but the **PATH** is different."

103. "The landing spot picks the club for you, but you see the ball rolling as far as the hole."

104. "No. I teach about motion."

105. "The upper body is stacked over the lower body. Have you ever seen this in reverse?"

106. "The game of golf will be a lot more fun if you remember that you are human and you are going to make mistakes."

1. IF THERE IS ONE NEGATIVE THING, THEN DON'T USE IT.

Manuel learned to teach golf from his father, Angel de la Torre. This became a great collaboration, and they would discuss and try out any new things that they thought could benefit their students. Manuel told us that his father directed him, whenever he had a new technique that he might use in his teaching, to get out a sheet of paper and draw a line down the middle of the sheet. He was to write all of the positive things that this new idea would have for the students on the left side of the paper and write all of the negative things that might happen on the right side of the paper. Manuel said that his father then told him, "If there is one negative thing, then don't use it."

This is one of the primary differences between Manuel's teaching and almost all other teachers. He felt this principle was so important that he cites it in the "Dedication" section that starts off his book, *Understanding the Golf Swing*. He writes that "when a student was told to do something, the more the student did it the better the results were to be. Nothing should be told to a student that could be over-done…"

It is clear that Manuel takes the teacher – student relationship so seriously that he never wants to tell the student to do something that could create problems in the future. Manuel is interested in working with principles that have been working for many years and will continue to work after all of the golfers of today are long gone.

• •

2. THE ARTISTRY IN THIS GAME IS GONE.

Manuel's father, Angel de la Torre, was the first Spanish golf professional. Angel won the Spanish Open for the first time in 1916, and the last of his seven wins came in 1935. He was the golf professional at the Real Club de la Puerta de Hierro on the outskirts of Madrid. It was on October 6, 1921, in the apartment above the golf shop that Manuel was born. Manuel and his father had one of the most wonderful partnerships ever formed in the game of golf - Father and son, accomplished players, and two of the greatest teachers in the game.

During a seminar for golf professionals, Manuel will often refer to things said to him by his father and the discussions that he and his father had about ways to improve their teaching of golf. In one seminar, Manuel was bemoaning the fact that all of the shots on the Tour had become full shots flown to the hole. The players want to have so many wedges so they have a club for every shot. Manuel said, "My father shot 61 with 5 clubs! The artistry in this game is gone."

Manuel does not often hearken back to "the good old days." His teaching is about principles that will apply to any person or any era, and he has mentioned several times that he is pleased that the current golf professionals seem more willing to listen to new and different ideas about teaching golf.

· ·

3. THE CLUB DOESN'T ACCELERATE; IT IS A DEAD OBJECT.

Manuel changed the words used by his father and Ernest Jones, the legendary golf teacher from England, who wrote *Swing the Clubhead*. In the Ernest Jones principles one is asked to swing the club**head** using the **hands**. Manuel changed the words with regard to the forward swing, asking the student to swing the **whole** club from the end of the backswing to the finish, using the **arms**. (This is the strict definition of the arms meaning the part of the extremity from the shoulder to the elbow, not the forearm.) Manuel made this change in wording soon after accepting the position as Head Golf Professional at the Milwaukee Country Club in 1951. He felt that many of these new students were not reacting as well to being asked to use the hands on the forward swing. They would cast the clubhead using leverage rather than a swinging motion. "I saw one of the workers on the golf course driving posts into the ground [try driving a post into the ground using a sledge hammer and you will feel the use of the arms to deliver the blow], and I thought of changing the words to, 'using the arms.' I tried it and it gelled."

Inevitably in the seminars Manuel will be asked what the golfer can do to hit the ball farther. The answer will be to increase the arm speed. One discussion on this topic found someone talking about the club doing this and the club doing that. Manuel seemed to want to bring the responsibility back to the golfer. He said, "The **club** does not accelerate; it is a dead object. The arms accelerate."

4. HIT EVERY SHOT WITHIN THAT TRIANGLE.

When Manuel was young, his father told him to begin a practice session by hitting 3 balls, and to look at the spot where those 3 balls landed because they would form a triangle. Then he was instructed to hit all of the practice shots with that club within the triangle. This same procedure was to be applied when changing clubs, including the driver. This was done primarily to get the student to avoid trying to hit the ball farther and farther. The tendency, when the student hits a number of good shots, is to then try to hit the ball harder and farther, thus ruining a good practice session.

Manuel told us about the "triangle of balls" practice idea, and related this story: "My Dad was watching me practice,

○ ~ 3

and I was hitting the shots well. Then I began hitting a few shots beyond the target, and he told me to stop practicing. 'You're done for the day.'" In a similar vein, Manuel mentioned that a lady had called him to book a lesson, and she said she wanted to be taught to hit the ball farther. In order to change this mindset Manuel responded, "Ma'am, I teach quality, not distance."

:::

5. WHAT DO YOU USE TO PUSH THE SCREW INTO A PIECE OF HARD WOOD? WHAT DO YOU USE TO TURN THE SCREW?

In Manuel's concept the player is told to use the hands to swing the clubhead to the end of the backswing and then to use the arms (the section from the shoulder to the elbow) to swing the whole club to the finish in the direction of the target. All too often the player uses the hands in the forward swing in an attempt to manipulate the clubface, and this twisting almost always puts the clubface in an incorrect position for a straight shot.

Manuel often uses examples from everyday life to get the student to understand. In order to help one student understand the different actions that come from the arms as opposed to the hands, Manuel said, "Suppose that you need to get a screw started into a piece of hard wood. What do you use?" Manuel will spend as much time as is needed to get the student to reason out the answer. He has often said that he does not ask all of these questions to embarrass the student, but he does want them to think and to remember.

"Yes, you push the point of the screw into the hard wood with your arm because this requires a good bit of force. Once you have the screw started, then what do you use to screw it into the wood? You use the hand because it is good at twisting things. The hands are good for turning screw drivers, but they can really distort the clubface if during the forward swing in golf."

....

6. WHAT ARE YOU TRYING TO DO?

No student will take a lesson with Manuel without being asked a question. There are dozens of possible questions that may be asked, and all are designed to get the student to really think about what is going on when he or she is playing a golf shot. These questions will lead to an understanding of the golf swing and may lead the student to an understanding of himself that he did not expect during a golf lesson.

One of Manuel's simplest questions can often be one of his most challenging and revealing questions. After some general discussion at the beginning of the lesson about the trend in shots that the student will hit, Manuel often asks, "What are you trying to do?"

In trying to answer this question, the student may first realize that he has no picture, or, at best, not a very clear picture of what it is that he is supposed to be doing. The student will often respond to Manuel's question by saying, "What do you mean? I am trying to hit a good shot straight at the target." If this is the response, then Manuel will try to get him to shift from thinking about the results to thinking about "the procedure that you use to get the ball to fly to the target." The student may now realize that he has never made the leap from trying to inflict his will on that little golf ball, to having a clear and consistent procedure for moving the golf club.

To force the student to deal with the procedure of the swing, Manuel may follow-up by asking the student, "What would you tell me to do if, I had never played golf before, and I asked you what I needed to do to play this shot?"

After the discussion that ensues from answering the question ["What are you trying to do?"], the student will be able to discard many things that are either unnecessary or incorrect. He may be able to begin to stop battling fears and expectations that only interfere with the natural ability to produce the golf swing. By the end of the lesson, the student will have a clearer picture of what he needs to do to build a swing that will work, even though, as a human being, he will not always get to do what he wants to do. But he can now have the belief, "If I do it, it works."

· ·

7. MY FATHER'S PARTING WORDS WERE ALWAYS, "OBSERVE YOURSELF."

A lesson with Manuel is always filled with questions, and he always wants the student to accept responsibility for **learning** the golf swing. One man commented to Manuel as another golf season was beginning, "Well, Manuel. Are you going to lower my handicap this year?" He responded, "No sir. I cannot do that." This was certainly not the answer that this gentleman was expecting, but Manuel went on to make his point.

"If I could hit the shots for you and post my scores for you, then I could lower your handicap, but since the rules do not allow me to do that, then **you** will have to work on your swing to get the improvement."

This type of thinking was introduced to Manuel early on by his father. Manuel often asks his students after a swing, "Do you feel the difference?" His father too had a common directive for Manuel after working with him. "My father's parting words were always, "Observe yourself." And it may be comforting to know that Manuel will often explain to the student that this is not an easy task. He said, "There are not too many things in your life that you have to observe that move as fast as a golf club."

8. DO YOU KNOW HOW I CAN TELL THAT YOU ARE NOT TARGET ORIENTED?

Once a player's swing has developed into a fairly good action, Manuel will often work with the player on directing the swing to the target. The concept calls for the golfer to swing the whole club from the end of the backswing to the finish **in the direction of the target**. Manuel will say, "The swing looks pretty good, but you are not giving it the correct direction."

He was working with one student on trying to "see the club on target before you ever start the backswing." On some swings he would say, "No, you went for the ball," and the shot would be off-line. He has said, "I want you to be 100% target oriented club-wise, not ball-wise." After a series of shots, some correct and some not, he asked, "Do you know how I can tell that you are not target oriented?" After a good bit of guessing and missing the answer, Manuel brought the student to a long rope stretched on the ground that was used to define the hitting area on the practice range. He explained that, as the club approached the ball, the shaft would point on the target line (in this case represented by the rope on the ground), and it would continue to point on the target line until it became level with the ground past the ball where it would be parallel to the target line. Manuel could see the club leave this line and that was his clue that the student's intent of getting the club on target had been lost. In this case the club would go left of the target line. The student's first reaction was to try to have the shaft continue to point to the target line during the forward swing, but Manuel said "no" to this complicated procedure–the student should simply "see" the club going on-target, and the club would do the correct thing in getting there.

9. I HAVEN'T TRIED TO MAKE A PUTT FOR OVER 40 YEARS.

Manuel preferred that the golfer have a different focus in putting versus the full swing. In putting the intent is to **roll the ball on the line as far as the hole**, so the focus has shifted to the ball. In the full swing the golfer should focus on the club and swinging the whole club from the end of the backswing to the finish with no ball concern. There are times when Manuel will work with golfer's putting stroke if he feels there is a major flaw, but, as soon as possible, the focus will return to rolling the ball.

"If you roll the ball on your line as far as the hole, what will happen? **IT** will go in the hole. **YOU** don't make it go in the hole." An attitude of simply rolling the ball is much different from that of trying to make the putt. Trying to hit the ball into the hole can produce a very different action from trying to simply roll the ball on the line. Regardless of the situation, whether it was the U.S. Open or a casual round, Manuel would encourage you to have the same purpose – to visualize the ball rolling on your line as far as the hole if it is a straight putt, or to a point left or right of the hole if it's a breaking putt. This visualization should exist prior to starting the stroke. Manuel said that his father called this type of thinking, "being realistic." It also happens to work better. Manuel once told a group of students, "I haven't tried to make a putt for over 40 years."

10. I DON'T TEACH POSTURE; BODIES ARE TOO DIFFERENT.

Manuel writes in his book, "When you place the clubhead behind the golf ball, be yourself and look like yourself. This means be natural. Don't stick any part of your body out in any direction if it doesn't usually stick out." You will rarely see Manuel dictate a posture change in an individual. He may push the hands and the grip-end of the club down slightly in the address position and ask the golfer to move his feet a little closer to the ball. In this case he would say that the golfer was too far from the ball at address, not that the golfer's posture was wrong.

"Our bodies are very smart. They will always respond correctly if we let them," said Manuel, "and this response will be different for different bodies." The body will always respond better if it's in a comfortable mode.

Manuel wants balance at the address position with 50% of the weight on the left foot and 50% on the right. He also wants the weight evenly divided from the heels to the toes, but when it comes to describing the correct posture for a golfer, "I don't teach posture. Bodies are too different."

● ●

11. ALWAYS THINK OF *BOTH* SHOULDERS TURNING.

One golfer was saying that he was trying to turn his left shoulder in the backswing, and Manuel explained, "Don't pick just one shoulder in turning because the left shoulder can go around the right shoulder using it as a pivot point, and this will give an incorrect turn." He is always on the lookout for the loose phrase that could be misinterpreted or could be overdone and then lead to other problems.

Try to turn your left shoulder back using the right shoulder as a pivot point, and then try turning your right shoulder back using the left shoulder as a pivot point. You can sense that these are two very different movements. In the first case you will lose your center away from the target and toward your toes during the backswing. In the second case you will lose your center to the target and toward your heels with this backswing turn. In terms of allowing your shoulders to respond in the backswing, Manuel said, "Always think of **both** shoulders turning."

....

12. THE HIPS DO THREE THINGS.

The de la Torre concept asks the golfer to be aware of the club while the body responds to that motion. He has often said that the hips do three things during the golf swing: "they **slide**, they **tilt**, and they **turn**." "Do the hips tilt more during the swing with a driver or with the swing of a sand iron?" Manuel would wait for the golfer to sense that the hips would do more tilting in response to the more vertical swing of the sand iron, and the hips would do more turning during the more horizontal swing with the driver. "Now you will have to be pretty smart to figure out the percentage difference in the sliding, tilting and turning of the hips for all of the different clubs," said Manuel. This was his plea to have the golfer just allow the hips to respond to the motion rather than trying to manage these movements.

....

13. NEVER JUST TELL THEM THE CLUB IS LAID-OFF; TELL THEM THE CAUSE.

There was a discussion during a PGA of America teaching seminar that Manuel was instructing about the golfer whose club is pointing well to the left of the target at the end of the backswing when the shaft was level with the ground. In this position the golfer is said to be "laid-off." Manuel was against just showing the student this incorrect position on video, and then showing them another golfer with the correct position where the shaft was parallel to the target line when level with the ground at the end of the backswing. "Never just tell them the club is 'laid-off'; tell them the cause," he implored. In this case the cause was **left-hand dominance** in the backswing. Both hands should be used equally during the backswing, but if the left hand begins to take over with the right hand giving up during the backswing, then the left hand will begin using the right hand like a fulcrum, and the club will have a leverage action (both ends of the club moving in different directions) rather than a swinging motion (both ends of the club moving in the same direction at the same time, and at the same rate of acceleration). This can occur at any point in the backswing, and it will force the club off the correct plane. The first time the club reaches level with the ground during the backswing, the shaft should be parallel to the target line with the toe of the clubhead pointing upward. If left-hand dominance has occurred, then the butt of the grip will point to the right of the target (rather than being parallel to the target line and therefore slightly left of the target), and the clubface will often point to the sky. The solution is to have the right hand continue working equally with the left hand during the entire backswing. If the right hand works throughout the backswing, then the club will be parallel to the target line when it is level with the ground (correct).

Why does the left hand tend to dominate during the backswing? Because it is moving in its "strong direction" during the backswing, just as the right hand is moving in its "strong direction" during the forward swing. To show this Manuel will ask the student to slap his hand using their right hand, and then slap his hand using their left hand. In both cases the person will slap with their palm facing the thing to be slapped, and not with the back of the hand. Why? Because this is the strong direction for each hand.

14. DON'T LEAVE HERE SAYING, "DE LA TORRE SAYS THE BODY DOESN'T MOVE."

Manuel's concept asks the golfer to use both arms to swing the club, the whole club, from the end of the backswing to the finish in the direction of the target. This concept is NOT meant to be a description of all of the movements that take place during a golf swing. It is meant to be the purpose that the golfer should have that will produce the correct action for a golf shot.

During the discussions on this concept, some would misinterpret the words to mean that the body does not move during the golf swing. Nothing could be further from the truth. The concept is meant to direct your intent, in other words, what **you** try to do. There are many things that should happen **in response to** what you are trying to do. Manuel will have discussions about the correct response from the shoulders, the hips or the legs to the intent to swing the club forward to the finish. And the one awareness that Manuel will ask the golfer to have on the forward swing is to allow the right heel to come off the ground **in response**, just as you would if you are tossing a ball underhanded. He feels that this is the best way to get the correct body-response to the swing, if this normal response is inhibited for some reason.

Manuel feels that the Ernest Jones book, *Swing the Clubhead*, may have lost a few readers due to the photographs of Jones swinging the club, because his body-response was different because he had lost his right leg below the knee in World War I. Therefore the look of Ernest Jones' legs and hips at impact and beyond was not typical of the top players of the day. This was just the way that Jones had to respond to the swing because of his personal situation.

If a golfer said that Manuel's concept could not work because it involved just the arms, then he would explain that if **you** use the arms, then the body should respond in complete synchronization to this action. You don't **use** the body to move the club; it simply responds to your intent to use the arms to produce the forward swing. He would leave no doubt by saying, "Don't leave here saying, "de la Torre says the body doesn't move!"

15. DON'T LEAVE HERE SAYING, "DE LA TORRE WANTS THE BALL IN THE CENTER."

At the address position Manuel asks the golfer to place the clubhead in the center between the feet. The center between the feet is determined by a vertical line from the midpoint between the shoulders to the ground. The clubhead of all of the clubs is placed in this center, unless the golfer is playing a special shot or is on ground that is not level.

Where do I place the ball in my stance? To this question Manuel would answer, "Place the ball in front of the clubhead, and since two objects cannot occupy the same space, the clubhead will be in the center, and the ball will be forward of center." It was explained that the value of this address position is that this is the only way a golfer could be in perfect balance. Also, it is easy to have the shoulders parallel to the target line when the clubhead is placed in the center. (Manuel will explain that the shoulders and the target line are actually just on the same plane. Because the shoulders are not level at the address position, they are not actually parallel to the target line.)

If you have the driver placed forward in the stance, then this tends to have the shoulder plane directed to the left; and if you have the short irons placed back in the stance, then the shoulder plane is directed to the right. This variation will also promote two different directions for the backswing with the driver tending to go back outside the correct path and the short iron tending to go back inside the correct path. Manuel might conclude this discussion by asking, "What is it that you want your shots to be … more than anything?" **Consistent**, would be the answer. So, how does changing the clubhead position for all of the different clubs help to promote consistency for your game?

While looking at the club at address, one should check both ends of the club independently. Check that the clubhead is in the center and then check that the grip end of the shaft points to the center of the body. Manuel explained that because the right hand is lower than the left, therefore the right shoulder is lower than the left, and this puts the head slightly back of center. In the correct address position the grip end of the shaft may appear ahead of center because the head is slightly back of center. So simply check that the grip end points to the center of the body.

Manuel's suggestion to place the clubhead in the center with **all** clubs is one that seemed very controversial. Someone would often object to this point saying that he just doesn't think he can put the ball in the center for the driver. He will remind them that the ball is forward of center; it is only the clubhead that is in the center. "Don't leave here saying, 'de la Torre wants the ball in the center,'" said Manuel.

. . . .

16. MY DAD NEVER ASKED WHAT I SHOT.

"My Dad never asked what I shot," said Manuel. The point here was to focus on how many times that he made the correct swing, and that making good swings was the only thing that the golfer should be focused on. Manuel once said to us, "If you are going to the golf course to shoot a low score, then you might as well just stay home." Especially for serious tournament players Manuel would ask these questions: "Who wins the tournament?" (That is the person who takes the fewest number of strokes.) "Who takes the fewest number of strokes?" (That is the person who makes the greatest number of good swings.) So you can see that good swings leads to fewer strokes which lead to success in tournaments. "Can you ever reverse this sequence?" asked Manuel.

Manuel told us that his Dad would ask him how he had played, "and that meant, how many times did I swing the club the way he had taught me," said Manuel.

··

17. THE WRISTS HINGE ON THE PLANE.

Manuel was explaining that the wrists hinge on the plane of the backswing. He was asked since the wrists hinge in the upward direction, if the hands were the same at the top of the backswing as they were at address except for the wrist hinge. "No. They (the wrists) hinge **on the plane**. What if you swing around behind you like in baseball? The wrists hinge on that plane which would be different than a vertical swing directly over your head," said Manuel.

The question here was directed at whether the back of the left hand was flat with the left forearm or bent ("cupped') at the end of the backswing. To see how the back of your left hand will be at the end of the backswing, simply swing the clubhead over your right shoulder and stop. There will be a slightly different left-hand position every time that you would change the plane of the swing, as in the horizontal plane of the baseball swing, the vertical swing of a sledge hammer that goes directly over the head, or the golf swing that goes over the right shoulder.

··

18. I DON'T CARE ABOUT THE LENGTH OF THE BACKSWING AS LONG AS THE HANDS ARE QUIET.

One of the reasons that a backswing can get too long is that the player is trying to get a greater cocking action of the wrists at the end of the backswing. Manuel has worked with golfers to reduce the size of the backswing, but not because there is some inherent problem with a long backswing. In fact, he has encouraged an ample backswing so there is plenty of space to produce speed. However, in the case where the hands add something in the backswing that is not part of a swinging motion, he has asked for a shorter backswing. At the heart of the matter is detecting the difference between the **swinging motion** where both ends of the club, the butt of the grip and the clubhead, are moving together in the same direction at the same time, and the **leverage action** (an error) where both ends of the club go in opposite directions. The mistake of leverage can occur if the hands suddenly flip the clubhead downward at the end of the backswing. This sudden jolt to the swing now puts the club out of position, and what was flipped out of position must be "unflipped" at some point to return the clubface back to square by impact.

To allow a golfer to feel the correct way to use the hands to produce the backswing, Manuel will ask the golfer to go from the address position and simply set the club on the right shoulder. This should be a very gradual and continuous movement with no sudden bursts of speed. The hands should not do all the work at the beginning of the backswing, nor should they wait until the very end to wind up the coil.

The length of each golfer's backswing will vary with his flexibility. "I don't care about the length of the backswing as long as the hands are quiet," said Manuel.

• •

19. IN A PLATOON OF MARCHING SOLDIERS, WHO MOVES FIRST? WHO LEADS?

The question will often come up regarding what is the first move from the top, or what is leading on the forward swing. Though these questions appear to be similar, they are actually very different. The quick answer that Manuel will give to what moves first is **"nothing."** If you ask, does the left hip lead the arms on the forward swing, then Manuel would say, yes it does. You might take that answer about what is leading and feel that you should move your left hip first to begin the forward swing, but do not do this. This will cause problems with your golf swing.

You should use both arms to swing the whole club forward to the finish in the direction of the target. This does **NOT** mean that the arms move first either. So, what moves first from the top? **NOTHING!** Everything moves together in complete unison. In a perfect swing, you will see the movement of the arms and the hips beginning at the same time in the forward swing. You could say that the use of the arms to swing the club forward will **trigger** everything, but the hips should respond at the same instant.

Yet the hips lead the arms on the forward swing. Once the coil of the backswing has been wound up, the left hip is simply closer to the destination of the forward swing than are the arms. And the arms are closer than the hands, etc. all down the chain. Manuel explained it this way: "In a platoon of marching soldiers – who moves first? Nobody. They all begin marching at the same time. Who leads? The soldiers in the front of the line will lead.

....

20. DOES AN INFIELDER IN BASEBALL TAKE A STEP BACKWARD BEFORE THROWING THE BALL?

Manuel will tell you to keep your weight equal, 50% left and 50% right, from address all the way until impact, and then allow the motion to shift the weight to the left foot after impact. This will get the attention of many golfers who feel that they should shift the weight to the right foot on the backswing. Why should this weight be shifted on the backswing? The answer comes back that you need to shift to the right so you can get power on the forward swing. Manuel would ask these questions: "Does an infielder in baseball take a step backward before throwing the ball? When you want to drive your car forward, do you drive in reverse first before going forward? Do you take a step backward before walking forward?" Often, after asking this last question, Manuel would take one step back and then begin walking forward. Nobody who saw this could help but smile at the thought of people walking around all day by taking one step back before walking forward.

Someone might produce a picture of one of the tour players who has noticeably shifted to the right in the backswing. (You could look at Tour players such as Ben Hogan, Jack Nicklaus or Steve Elkington who do not shift to the right.) Manuel will often point out two things: first is that he does not like to use Tour players as examples because they are very talented and they practice quite a bit more than the average golfer. "They can stand on their heads and hit good shots," he said. The second point is the principle that, if you displace your center to the right by shifting the weight in the backswing, then you must reestablish that center at the point of impact. And this will take a great deal of timing and practice with no benefit.

· ·

21. WHAT WAS THE PRESIDENT'S NAME IN 1952?

A group of golf instructors went to dinner with Manuel after one of his teaching seminars. The discussion came to the importance of using just the right word in golf instruction. You need to select words that have the fewest possible different interpretations so the student does not get the wrong picture. Manuel recommends asking the students to sum up their lesson near the end so he or she will know if their interpretation is correct.

Manuel recalled one lesson where his student was very "violent" at the ball, so he told the student to swing the club from the end of the backswing to the finish in one movement, only concerned with getting the club to the finish. Manuel saw the student later and asked him how he did.

"I never hit one good shot, but I remembered what you told me," said the student.

So Manuel asked him, "What were you trying to do?"

"I was trying to swing through the ball just like you told me," he replied.

Manuel then told us, "Here I spent an entire lesson trying to make the golf ball disappear, and what did this man do when he went to play. He put it right back in as big as ever."

We were not told this lesson story to belittle the student, but rather to make us diligent as instructors to have the student totally clear on what was to be done. Manuel then asked us, as we waited for our dinner, "What was the President's name in 1952?" We all quickly narrowed it down to Harry S Truman or Dwight D. Eisenhower.

Manuel waited and gave the correct answer, "No, Bill Clinton (the current President). That is his name now, and that was his name in 1952. I did not ask, who was the President in 1952."

. . . .

22. THROW A BASEBALL OVERHAND, AND NOW THROW A BASEBALL SIDEARM. DOES THE BODY MOVE DIFFERENTLY FOR EACH THROW?

"Throw a baseball overhand, and now throw a baseball sidearm. Does the body move differently for each throw? Of course it does. Now did you think about the different body movements, or did you just use your arm differently?" asked Manuel. This discussion is used to encourage the student to simply use the arms to swing the club and to allow the body to respond to that action. Manuel likes to use everyday, commonplace activities to take the individual out of the golf-mentality that often has the average golfer tied in knots trying to control hips, legs, shoulders, etc.

This is not to say that Manuel does not discuss, in great detail, what might happen if a golfer tried to move in different ways. He will do this with aspiring golf teachers, and he will tell them to "try these things for themselves."

"Try these things that golfers try to do and see what the effects are," said Manuel.

It always comes back to the simplicity of trying to swing the club properly and allowing the body to respond to the motion.

· ·

23. WHERE IS THE MUSCLE MEMORY?

When somebody insists that he has "muscle memory" for the golf swing, Manuel will ask him to come up and then address the golf ball. At this point he will remain silent for as long as it takes until the person becomes impatient in the address position.

"Where is the muscle memory? Why didn't you hit the shot?" asks Manuel.

"You didn't ask me to swing; I didn't think I was supposed to swing," he will say. Manuel will respond, "If the muscles had memory, then they would move the moment they feel the club."

Manuel will explain that, before any swing will take place, an image has to form in the mind of what is to be done. Everything starts in the mind before any muscles go into action. There is no muscle in the body that has a brain.

In one lesson with Manuel, a student had reached a point where the shots were flying great. In his exuberance he asked Manuel, "How long will it be before I don't have to think about it?"

"When you're dead, then you won't have to think about it. Until that time your mind will have to work to set the swing in motion," said Manuel.

* *

24. WHY DO WE TAKE A DIVOT?

In Manuel's concept the golfer is asked to swing the club **forward**, not downward. Then the question comes up that, if the swing is truly forward, why do we often take a divot? Manuel first explains that a correct divot will be symmetrical, meaning that it will gradually get deeper and then will gradually come out of the ground. This type of divot is still level with the ground even though the clubhead cuts below the surface. An incorrect divot will continue on a sharp downward angle.

This still does not answer the question of why the clubhead, which was just resting on top of the grass at address, will get below the surface after impact in a swing that is forward. Manuel explained that this is because the knees increase their flex in response to the forward swing. This increase in the knee flex drops the golfer's center slightly, which results in the clubhead taking a divot. The correct divot also takes place on the target-side of the ball, not back of the ball.

Manuel would often caution the golfer, "Don't try to take a divot. If the clubhead takes a divot, that is fine."

* *

25. THE SHOULDERS *START* WITH, *STAY* WITH, AND *STOP* WITH THE CLUBHEAD IN THE BACKSWING.

If the golfer's shoulders are not responsive in the backswing, or if they start off synchronized with the clubhead but then stop turning, Manuel will tell the student to have "the shoulders **start** with, **stay** with, and **stop** with the clubhead in the backswing. It is important that the shoulders are **responding** to the swinging of the clubhead in the backswing and the golfer is NOT trying to use the shoulders to produce the backswing. It is also important that the mind is on both the clubhead and the shoulders as they move in unison. To emphasize this last point, Manuel will have a person extend both arms and point both index fingers straight out. Now he will instruct the person to move both index fingers up and down in unison. "Your mind cannot be on just one of the fingers to have them move in unison; it must be on both fingers at the same time," he said.

Reducing the body's response on the backswing is one of the causes of slicing that is outlined in Manuel's book, *Understanding the Golf Swing.* When the body's response is stifled, the shoulder turn is reduced, and this will cause the club to approach the ball from "outside in" on the forward swing, thus causing the slice.

When this problem occurs, then Manuel asks the golfer to have the shoulders **start** with, **stay** with, and **stop** with the clubhead during the backswing. He calls this a "corrective procedure," and, as soon as possible, the golfer should get his thought back on the forward swing.

· ·

26. USING THE ARMS DOES NOT MEAN YOU USE MUSCULAR STRAIN.

Using the arms to swing the golf club from the end of the backswing to the finish does not require great physical power. The club weighs less than a pound, and to produce speed, the golfer must remain very free of muscular tension. "If you had to suddenly walk faster, would you stiffen your legs? If you wanted to throw a baseball far, would you stiffen your arm?" asks Manuel. Of course not. This would not be natural.

If the golfer makes the common mistake of "casting" or throwing the clubhead using the hands during the forward swing, then Manuel will ask him or her to give the responsibility to the arms for producing the forward swing. Then Manuel will often caution the golfer saying, "Using the arms does not mean you use muscular strain." Using the arms rather than the hands does not mean that you have to become stiff, or full of effort and strain. You simply **use** your arms in a very free and flexible way, as you would in throwing a baseball.

· ·

27. IF YOU *USE* YOUR ARMS, YOU ARE NOT *USING* YOUR SHOULDERS.

In Manuel's concept you **use** your arms to swing the club forward. Your shoulders move, but you should not **use** them; your hips move, but you should not **use** them. Your hands, wrists and feet will move, but you should not **use** them to produce the forward swing.

If you use the shoulders in a turning action from the end of the backswing, then the club will come outside the correct direction on the forward swing, and the golfer will slice the ball. The correction is to give the responsibility for the forward swing back to the arms and let the shoulders simply respond. It does not mean that you hold the shoulders back; they will move during the forward swing. It means that you do not **USE** them.

"If you **use** your arms, you are not **using** your shoulders," said Manuel.

· ·

28. I VERY SELDOM CHANGE THE SPEED OF A PERSON'S BACKSWING.

"I do not like to see a sharp or sudden move away from the target in the backswing," said Manuel. He would explain to the golfer that the backswing is just a "prepara-tory movement" to get the club in place for the forward swing. The speed of the backswing has nothing to do with the speed that will be produced on the forward swing, so there should be no rush to get the club back.

"Take your address position. Now simply set the club on your right shoulder without thinking about golf." This is a method that Manuel would use to see the proper speed for a particular golfer's backswing.

Every individual will have his or her own tempo for the backswing, and that tempo may change from day to day. "I very seldom change the speed of a person's backswing," said Manuel.

....

29. WHY DOES THE RIGHT ARM SUPPLY MORE OF THE SPEED ON THE FORWARD SWING?

The discussion during one of the golf teaching seminars came around to the right arm vs. the left arm and which one supplies more of the speed in the golf swing. Manuel explained that while both arms need to be used, the lead arm sets the radius for the swing, but the trailing arm sup-plies more of the speed. Then he asked, "Why does the right arm supply more of the speed on the forward swing?"

After the group took several complicated stabs at answer-ing the question, Manuel explained it this way: the right arm supplies more speed because it is **coiled** (the elbow is bent) at the end of the backswing, and the left arm is extended. If you saw a snake several feet away from you which was extended in a straight line, would you worry that it could suddenly strike and bite you? Would you be more worried if you saw a snake several feet away from you which was all coiled up? You should be more worried about the coiled snake!

30. WHEN I WANT TO SEND THE BALL FAR-THER, I DON'T THINK OF CLUBHEAD SPEED. I CONCERN MYSELF WITH ARM SPEED.

"If golfers could play the game of golf without concern for this word 'power,' everyone could improve his or her game at least 50%." This is how Manuel begins Chapter 10 of his book, *Understanding the Golf Swing*. But the questions of how to get more distance will often surface in any golf clinic. One junior golfer, who was making great progress during a lesson with Manuel, finally said she would like more distance. Manuel said that distance was like a flower. It grows gradually, almost without notice, as the golf swing improves, and this young lady should not concern herself with distance. Let this distance flower as the swing gets better and better. I can't say if she bought into this philosophy for the long-term, but it kept from ruining what had been good progress during this lesson.

When a golfer is struggling with casting the clubhead during the forward swing in an effort to hit hard, Manuel has said, "When I want to send the ball farther, I don't think of club**head** speed. I concern myself with arm speed."

This gets the student to have the correct sequence for the action. "You can't jump the speed directly into the clubhead," said Manuel. The arms must move faster, so the forearms move faster, so the hands move faster, so the grip moves faster, so the shaft moves faster, and so the clubhead moves faster. The golfer cannot skip any of the links in this chain.

Also notice that Manuel uses the words, "to send the ball farther," and not to **hit** the ball **harder**. So, to send the ball farther, the golfer needs to move his or her arms faster, and all parts of the body will need to move faster in response to the increase in arm speed.

"Remember, we all have our god-given limits in this department. If you try to go beyond what you have, then you will ruin the swing," cautioned Manuel.

31. THE HANDS SIMPLY HOLD IT. THE ARMS SWING IT.

Manuel has stated that the most frequent cause of problems in the swing is using the hands to cast the clubhead, thus creating a leverage action, rather than a swinging motion, going forward. In his concept, the golfer is asked to use both arms (the section from the shoulder to the elbow) to swing the whole club from the end of the backswing to the finish, in the direction of the target. So the golfer must understand that the hands do NOT have the job of producing any speed during the forward swing. If the hands try to produce speed, then the arm speed, and thus distance, will be reduced.

The hands do have a job with the club on the forward swing. "The hands simply hold it. The arms swing it," said Manuel. While the concept of using the arms has been very helpful for golfers, Manuel has said that you do not need to think about the arms if you know what a swinging motion really is.

32. WHEN YOUR ARMS STOP, THE CLUBHEAD CANNOT GET VERY FAR OUT THERE (TOWARD THE TARGET).

After a series of good swings during a lesson, one golfer said, "I feel the clubhead is farther out there [pointing toward the target] on the correct swing."

"When your arms stop [on the forward swing], the clubhead cannot get very far out there (toward the target)," responded Manuel.

To help with this problem, Manuel will hold the shaft of a golf club vertically against the ground, directly on the target line, just out of reach of the golfer's forward swing. Then he will ask the student to swing forward with the intent of having his clubhead actually touch the shaft that Manuel is holding on the target line, even though the golfer knows that his club cannot quite reach that shaft. This works wonders on getting the golfer to swing the club in the correct direction, namely forward to the target, rather than downward at the ball.

The golfer needs to keep the arms working on the forward swing to make the club swing forward to touch this shaft placed ahead on the target line. If the hands take over, or the action becomes so ball-directed that the arms stop when the club was in the ball area, then the club will not be so extended on the target line past the ball.

Manuel explains that the classic picture of the club extending down the target line after impact is something that the centrifugal force (outward pull) will produce. It is something that the swinging motion itself will do to the player **provided the player remains very flexible, with a lack of muscle tension**. This so-called extension is something that the swing will do to the golfer if he or she has the correct motion and maintains a lack of muscle tension during the swing. This extension is not something **the golfer** should try to produce. It just happens.

....

33. IN THE BACKSWING I USE MY HANDS. I DON'T GET INVOLVED WITH WHERE MY WRISTS HINGE.

Discussions about the backswing often get to questions about an early wrist cock versus a late wrist cock. In Manuel's concept the golfer is asked to swing the clubhead back with the hands toward the right shoulder. This should be a gradual and continuous action. What seems to be meant in the early wrist cock is that the hands complete the coil of the backswing very early on, and the late wrist cock has the hands inactive until near the end of the backswing. Neither of these methods would seem ideal, and it seems obvious that either one could be overdone and create problems of timing for the swing.

Make no mistake-there are good golfers that produce the backswing using one of these two methods, but as Manuel will say, these good golfers swing the club forward very well and they play and practice all the time. In the simplest action the hands are used during the entire backswing, so they do not need to do any extra work at the beginning or the end of the backswing.

Manuel will tell you that you should NOT try to cock your wrists during the backswing. The hands are used to swing the clubhead back, and the wrists are simply hinges that are cocked by the club swinging over the shoulder. The swinging motion will cock the wrists on the correct plane for that particular club if you will let it; if you try to cock the wrists, then you will likely get the club off the correct plane.

To feel the correct action, the golfer can go from the address position, forget about golf, and simply set the club on the right shoulder. Did you think about where and how to cock the wrist? "In the backswing I use my hands. I don't get involved with where my wrists hinge," said Manuel.

. . . .

34. THE MOMENT YOU ANTICIPATE THE RETURN TO THE BALL, YOU CUT OFF THE BACKSWING.

In one lesson Manuel was working with an older gentleman on trying to increase the length of the backswing. At first they used a 3-step process: Step 1 had the golfer go from the address position and set the shaft on the right shoulder, straight up in front of him, with the shaft horizontal and then stopping. Step 2 had the golfer go backward, as in the direction of the golf swing, and set the shaft on the right shoulder, being sure he let the shaft go horizontal to the ground and then stopping. Step 3 had him repeat Step 2, but to go ahead and swing forward and hit the shot. Manuel reminded him, "Don't just let the club **drop** to horizontal. **You** put it there."

Manuel also told him, "You have to decide to put the club horizontal the moment you leave the ball; you can't decide when you get near the top" (of the backswing).

This procedure to increase the size of a very restricted backswing was having some success, but you could see how everything changed when the golfer was going to swing forward to hit the shot. Step 1 and Step 2 were done with a backswing length that would have made this man very happy, but Step 3 was noticeably shorter.

"The moment you get in a hurry, the moment you anticipate the return to the ball, you cut off the backswing," said Manuel.

35. IN ANY SWING WHERE THE CLUB REACHES THE HORIZONTAL LEVEL PAST THE BALL, THE BACK FOOT SHOULD BE STRAIGHT UP.

The body should simply respond to the motion on the forward swing, and Manuel likes to work with the golfer's right foot if the body is not responding. Just as you should if you are throwing a ball underhand, let the right heel come up in response to the forward swing. The golfer's body should finish more vertically if he or she allows the right heel to come up.

"A player should be able to throw the golf club to the target if they wanted to," noted Manuel. He did caution that if you wanted to have someone actually throw the golf club at the target, to watch out because he may throw it over his left shoulder if he makes the mistake of casting the clubhead with the hands.

In the golf swing the body coils from the top down [backswing], but it uncoils from the bottom up [forward swing]. Manuel said this would be a good image to give a golfer to have him work with having the right heel come up in response to the forward swing.

Even on the little shots around the green, the golfer should let the right heel come up. This is a shot where a golfer can become very fixed and unresponsive, which makes it difficult to swing the club **forward**. Manuel went on to say, "In any swing where the club reaches the horizontal level past the ball, the back foot should be straight up."

36. *LET* THE CLUB GO TO ZERO (m.p.h.) IN THE BACKSWING.

Imagine you are swinging on a swing in the park. After you reach the end of one arc, you will begin to swing in the opposite direction where you slowly begin to build speed, and the speed will increase until you reach the midpoint of the arc. Then your ride will begin to gradually slow down until you again reach the end of the arc where, for a brief instant, you will be going zero miles per hour (m.p.h.). It is this type of ride that you should give your golf club, and it will propel the ball for you.

While working with one student, Manuel described the situation saying, "Sometimes you stop the club in the backswing to go forward. **LET** the club go to its conclusion in the backswing." He explained that, in order to stop the club on the backswing, you must get muscularly tight, and this was not good for producing the correct forward swing.

Several times Manuel has described the importance, and the difficulty, of the word - **LET**. The golfer is so anxious to control things that he or she will not **LET** the motion happen. It requires effort and tension to stop a club that is swinging, and this can destroy the timing and the speed of the swing.

In the case of this lesson, Manuel summed it up by saying, "**Let** the club go to zero (m.p.h.) in the backswing."

. . . .

37. THE HAND LEVEL WILL CHANGE AT THE TOP OF THE BACKSWING FROM CLUB TO CLUB BECAUSE OF THE DIFFERENT PLANES OF THE SWING.

Golfers love to talk about the swing plane. Manuel defines *plane* as the inclination of the circle the golf club makes when it is swung, with respect to the horizontal level of the ground. Whether it is with the driver or the sand wedge, the golfer is asked to swing the clubhead over the shoulder in the backswing. Because of the different lengths of the clubs, they obviously swing on different planes. Manuel said that checking the club when the shaft is perpendicular to the target line during the swing is a good place to check the plane. At this point the butt of the club should point at the target line to be considered on the correct plane. However, he would never ask the golfer to sense that the butt of the club is pointing at the target line. In fact, during a teaching seminar, he asked some of the professionals to try to put the club where the butt of the club pointed on the target line when perpendicular to it so they would see that they could not get it correct. If the golfer will just swing the clubhead over the shoulder, then he will be on the correct plane. In other words, the motion of the swing will find the correct plane, so just be concerned with producing the motion.

In fact, for those of us that love such details, Manuel said, "The hand level will change at the top of the backswing from club to club because of the different planes of the swing." So the hand level will be lower with a driver versus a sand wedge, because the plane of the driver is more horizontal than the sand wedge.

Manuel told of working with one of his Tour players that was swinging the sand wedge on the bunker shots as if it was on the swing plane of his driver. When the golfer swung the sand wedge to the shoulder in the backswing, on the correct plane for that club, the bunker shots were much better.

Conversely, if a golfer were trying to have his hands get to a higher level at the top of his backswing with a driver versus his sand wedge, then this could create problems with the driver. Just follow the concept and swing all of the clubs over the shoulder in the backswing, and they will find their correct plane without you fussing over it.

. . . .

38. I DON'T GET TOO INVOLVED WITH SAYING, 'USE THE HANDS IN THE BACKSWING,' BECAUSE THERE IS ONLY ONE WAY TO GET IT OVER THE SHOULDER.

In Manuel's concept of the full swing, the hands are used to swing the clubhead back to the end of the backswing over the shoulder. The hands are needed to "wind up the coil," so to speak, in the backswing. While working with a brand new golfer, Manuel will generally ask him or her to simply set the club on the right shoulder (for a right-handed golfer) and let the body respond to give him the feel of the backswing. Then he would have him set the club on the right shoulder and then elevate it several inches over the shoulder to get him to sense the correct destination for the backswing. Subsequently, the golfer could swing the club from the address position to where it is over the shoulder at the end of the backswing.

Occasionally, an individual may try to use the shoulders, the body, or the hips to produce the backswing. While these parts of the anatomy will move during the backswing, they cannot produce a sufficient coil that is needed for a full swing. Both hands are needed to produce the motion, and the wrists must remain flexible to respond to this motion of the club that is the backswing.

Quite often, Manuel would stress the need to use of the **arms** to produce the **forward** swing, but he did not often stress the need to use the **hands** on the **backswing**. He said, "I don't get too involved with saying, 'Use the hands in the backswing,' because there is only one way to get it [the club] over the shoulder."

39. EVEN IF I WANTED TO QUADRUPLE THE ARM SPEED ON THE FORWARD SWING, THE BACKSWING (SPEED) WOULD STAY THE SAME.

"What really is the purpose of the backswing," Manuel would ask. This discussion might take place if the student was putting too much speed and effort into the backswing. Manuel would explain, "The backswing is just a **preparatory movement** to get the club in place so you can swing it forward." If you intend to strike a hard blow with an ax or a hammer, do you speed up the "backswing," or the preparatory movement, in order to strike this harder blow? I hope that you do not.

To emphasize this point, Manuel said, "Even if I wanted to quadruple the arm speed on the forward swing, the backswing [speed] would stay the same."

40. ONCE YOU SET THE DIRECTION ON THE BACKSWING, KEEP GOING IN THAT SAME DIRECTION.

One student would begin the backswing by pushing the club away from him, and this would make the club go straight back. The clubhead should go in a circular direction away from the ball so, when the shaft becomes level with the ground, it is parallel to the target line. Manuel will often hold a club vertically with the butt of the grip against the ground on a spot about a foot and a half behind the ball on the target line. This will force the student's club to go in a circular direction at the start of the backswing, rather than being pushed away, straight back. Naturally, this change made the student feel that he was taking the club too far inside.

The impact on the shots became much better because the club was now on the correct plane from the beginning of the backswing, and the golfer did not need to make an in-swing correction. After several swings Manuel said, "Once you set the direction on the backswing, keep going in that same direction." He further explained by saying that, while the beginning of the backswing was now fine, the student then made the club go too upward to return to the "feel" that he was used to with his other backswing direction. "Once you go back on the circle [correct direction], keep going back in that direction. Don't change to **UP**," he said. These instructions from Manuel show his belief that, ideally, there was just one direction for the backswing, which is a circular pattern backward to the shoulder. There is no need for a series of directions and movements to perform the backswing.

Also, it is the **player** who sets this direction. That may sound obvious, but one student asked Manuel, "If I just produce a swinging motion in the backswing, will the club be going in the correct direction?" The answer is no, not necessarily.

• •

41. IF YOU WANT TO MAKE THE BACKSWING LONGER, THEN *EVERYTHING* GOES BACK FARTHER.

In one lesson the student was trying to achieve a longer backswing, which he was clearly capable of doing, but he was using his hands incorrectly near the end of the backswing. He would add a sudden effort with his hands, near the top, and this produced a leverage action (incorrect). You can detect leverage in the action when the clubhead end of the club and the grip end of the club move in opposite directions. In a swinging action, both ends of the club move in the same direction at the same time. You cannot have leverage and swinging in the same motion.

This student would flip the clubhead downward near the end of the backswing while the grip end of the club would pop upward. This was an effort to increase the size of the backswing, but the body was not responding. Manuel said, "If you want to make the backswing longer, then **everything** goes back farther." Yes the hands should continue the swinging motion, but the shoulders, the hips, and the feet will need to continue to respond if the backswing size is to increase without destroying what should be a swinging motion.

Manuel told the story that several years ago one student came to him and took the golf club and swung it over the shoulder where the club was level with the ground. He said to Manuel, "Do you see where this club is? I can't get it there!"

Manuel said to him, "You just did."

42. I PREFER TO HAVE THE PLAYER KEEP THE WEIGHT EQUAL (50% left and 50% right) THAN TO TRY TO STAY CENTERED.

"What is the first thing that you need to determine in order to draw a circle with a compass?" This is a question that Manuel will often ask to get the player to realize that he should not try to shift his weight to the right during the backswing. Manuel's answer to the question is, "You need to determine the center point." If you displace your center during the backswing, then you will need to reestablish it at the moment of impact in order for the club to return to square, and that is a fairly difficult thing to do. For simplicity, Manuel uses the midpoint between the shoulders as a point of reference for their "center." The exact point of this theoretical center is not important, and it is not some specific body part.

This geometry lesson leads to Manuel asking the student to "keep your weight equal, 50% left and 50% right, from the start of the backswing until impact." In this way, the player does not require the perfect timing of reestablishing the center at the same time that the club is returning to impact. Keep your weight equal until impact, and the center stays in the same location until impact. Then you should respond to the speed of the forward swing, and the center will move forward and upward after impact.

"I prefer to have the player keep the weight equal (50% left and 50% right) than to try to stay centered," Manuel said. He explained that some golfers tended to become tight and unresponsive in their turn when they tried to "stay centered." While the center should "stay in the same location" until impact, it should be allowed to pivot in response to the swing. Manuel feels that maintaining the center can best be handled by sensing it through the feet, and that keeping the weight 50% left and 50% right from start of the backswing until impact will not inhibit the free response of the golfer that should take place during the swing.

....

43. IF THE PLANE OF THE FILM THAT IS USED TO PHOTOGRAPH THE SWING IS PARALLEL TO THE ACTUAL PLANE OF THE SWING, YOU CAN SEE THE SHAPE OF THE SWING.

Manuel will point out that the arc of the forward swing is very close to being a perfect circle. The key is for the photographic image to be taken from the correct position. "If the plane of the film that is used to photograph the swing is parallel to the actual plane of the swing, you can see the shape of the swing," he explained.

Most times a golf swing is filmed from about chest-high to the golfer so the plane of the golf swing is tilted away from the camera, and, from this perspective, the arc of the forward swing appears to be an ellipse.

....

44. HOW CAN THE RIGHT HIP MOVE IF THE RIGHT KNEE DOESN'T MOVE?

One of the current golf instruction clichés is to keep the right knee still during the backswing. Sometimes it is just said that the right knee should remain flexed during the backswing, but it is often said to keep it absolutely motionless. Manuel would not agree with either of these directions. He would tell someone, who was facing forward, to turn and look over his right shoulder. "What did your right knee do? It straightened. What did your left knee do? Its flex increased," Manuel explained. He did not like the idea of creating resistance or tension in the body during the swing. The body should be left free to respond to the swing that was being produced.

Manuel explained that a person with a shorter trunk will need more hip turn, while a person with a very long trunk will need less hip turn to let the body turn in response to the swing. This is common sense, and most people will need a good amount of hip turn to allow the trunk to turn in response to a full backswing. So here is a player who is trying to achieve a big shoulder turn and a full backswing while keeping the right knee locked in place. Manuel will explain the natural way that the legs will move for a person who is turning to the right and encourage the individual to allow this to take place. To drive this point home Manuel asked, "How can the right hip move if the right knee doesn't move?" The bone connecting the knee to the hip cannot change in length, so for the hip to turn, the right knee must go along with it.

· ·

45. IN THE FORWARD SWING, THE CENTER GOES DOWN A LITTLE, BUT NOT FORWARD UNTIL AFTER IMPACT.

In discussing what the player's center did during the forward swing, Manuel explained that, ideally, the center will go downward a little because the knees compress during the forward swing in response to the action. This is why the club may take a small divot in the correct motion. He cautioned that taking a divot should never be a goal and that if **the swing** produced a divot, then that was fine. **The golfer** should not try to make a divot because he or she will likely go down rather than swinging forward. A correct divot should be symmetrical where it gets gradually deeper to its center and then gradually becomes shallower until the end of the divot. This shows that, while the clubhead may scrape off a layer of the turf, it is still moving forward and not downward.

The player's center should move forward in response to the forward swing only after impact. Manuel told the golf teachers that he would rather they tell the student that the **weight** moves to the left after impact rather than saying **you** go to the left. This phrasing let's the golfer know that the weight shift is something he should allow to happen in response to the swing instead of trying to make himself move to the left. If the golfer tries to figure out when to shift, he or she will mess up the timing."In the forward swing, the center goes down a little, but not forward until after impact," said Manuel.

46. I WOULD RATHER SEE A REVERSE-PIVOT (backswing), THAN MOVING OFF THE BALL (to the right) IN THE BACKSWING.

One of the common faults that is to be avoided at all costs, according to the current golf conversation, is the so called "reverse pivot." Here the golfer would lean toward the target during the backswing and would then move away from the target during the forward swing. Manuel really sees these as two separate problems. If the golfer actually moved away from the target during the forward swing, then this was usually an attempt to use the shoulders to try to get under the ball and get it up in the air. With this action the ball seldom got up in the air and was often "topped," where the leading edge of the clubhead met the top part of the ball, causing it to dribble along the ground. The solution to this problem is to get the player to understand that you cannot get under the ball if it is resting on the ground. It is the loft angle on the clubface that is responsible for giving the shot its trajectory, and the player needs to simply swing the club forward and brush the grass. If the body is allowed to respond to this forward motion, then it will move with the swing, and the weight will transfer toward the target. With this problem, Manuel will also work with the player's "mental picture." He wants the player to visualize the shot flying low, along the ground, on a straight line to the target. This will eliminate the desire to get the ball up into the air.

As for the backswing problem where the player will lean toward the target during the backswing, Manuel asked this question, "What will happen if I have a "reverse pivot" during the backswing, and I just swing the club forward?"

"All that will happen is that I will hit the ball a little lower" was his answer. In fact, addressing the ball with the player's center ahead of the ball is a way to hit a lower shot. To produce this lower shot, you can have the player put the ball back in the stance and swing forward. Manuel did not want to see the player's center get displaced toward the target during the backswing. However, he saw this as less of a problem than when a player moves backward to the right during the backswing, because now the player must move the center forward during the forward swing in order to get good contact. This requires very good timing which would come from a lot of practice that the average player will not do, and this shifting backward and shifting forward gives no benefits.

"I would rather see a 'reverse pivot' [backswing], than moving off the ball [to the right] in the backswing," said Manuel.

- -

47. WHY ARE THE HIPS TURNED TOWARD THE TARGET ("open") AT IMPACT? BECAUSE THE BODY UNCOILS FROM THE BOTTOM UP.

The prevalence of video and photographs in golf instruction has left the golf student with so many images of what he or she thinks should be happening in the golf swing.

When Manuel asks the golfer to simply swing the whole club from the end of the backswing to the finish using the arms, some golfers feel that they must do more to hit the shot. In one case, the question was, "Manuel, why are [insert Jones, Hogan, Palmer, Nicklaus or Woods] hips so 'open' at impact if all he is doing is using his arms?"

"Why are the hips turned toward the target ['open'] at impact? Because the body uncoils from the bottom up," answered Manuel. He explains that the body will coil from the top down (backswing), but will uncoil from the bottom up (forward swing). In relating this to golf he said that at the address position there is no coil, and then we wind up the coil during the backswing. At the end of the backswing, the left hip is closer to the target than the club in terms of the circular pattern of this coil. The left hip and the club are unified during the forward swing, so the left hip will remain closer to the target (leading) during the forward swing for quite a while, depending on the individual and his motion.

One must remember that Manuel will say that certainly the hips move during the forward swing, but the hips should move in response to the golfer's intent to move the golf club. The golfer should not try to **USE** his or her hips to produce the speed of the swing. To dramatize this Manuel will ask the golfer to hold the club out in front of him and place the clubhead in Manuel's hand, which was held several feet above the ground. "Now, when I tell you, I want you to move your hips very quickly toward the target. Are you ready? Go!" he will say. Then he will ask the student [with the clubhead still resting in the palm of Manuel's hand], "How much speed did you produce?" Manuel would then ask the golfer to check the clubface to see what had happened to it. The clubface would be "open," or facing to the right. He also said that, if you just used the hips to begin the forward swing, the plane of the club would become more horizontal ("flat").

One well-known drawing in Ben Hogan's famous book, *The Modern Fundamentals of Golf*, has a line connecting the golfer's left hand to the hips, and it encourages the use of the hips to begin the forward swing. Manuel told us, "I wish he had said that the club and the hips are UNIFIED in the forward swing – that they move together," rather than giving the sense that the golfer should use his or her hips to try to move the golf club.

....

48. DON'T FORCE THE RIGHT FOOT UP. LET IT GO. YOUR RIGHT LEG SHOULD BE VERY RELAXED.

The arms are used to produce the forward swing. The right heel is what Manuel wants you to use to "trigger" the body's response to the forward swing. Now the right heel need not be mentioned at all if the golfer was allowing the body to respond, and this is the ideal situation. If things were not responding enough, and this will occur more often on the small pitch shots, then Manuel will discuss allowing the right heel to come up in response to the forward swing. "Take this ball in your right hand. Now toss it underhand to that flagstick," he once said. When the golfer finished, Manuel grabbed him and told him to "stay there." The golfer was asked to notice how the right heel had come up in response when he tossed the golf ball.

Manuel emphasizes that this response from the right foot is not done with a great deal of exertion. It is done in a similar fashion to when you are standing and then you turn and begin walking to your left. The right heel just comes up in response.

One student was working on this, and he was using a sudden effort with the right foot. "Don't force the right foot up. Let it go. Your right leg should be very relaxed," Manuel said. He told us that at the finish of the swing, the teacher should be able to push on the golfer's right leg, and it should be very relaxed and supple, not straight and stiff.

49. IF YOU KEEP YOUR RIGHT KNEE FLEXED, YOU RESTRICT YOUR TURN.

Manuel explains what the legs do during the backswing by having a person stand normally, and then turn and face to the right. He will then ask, "What did the right knee do?" It will straighten as you turn. "If you keep your right knee flexed, you restrict your turn [in the backswing]," said Manuel.

He says that if you keep the right knee flexed and try to turn more during the backswing, then you will have to tilt the upper body to the right, and this will lead to the problem of moving the player's center. The player's center will then have to be reestablished at impact, and this is difficult to time properly.

50. DOES THE RIGHT ELBOW GET CLOSER TO THE RIGHT HIP DURING THE FORWARD SWING? NO, IT DOESN'T.

One discussion was dealing with the common golf tip that tells the player to drop the right elbow to the right hip at the start of the forward swing. Manuel does not like this because it is an exaggeration. If you truly dropped the right elbow into the right hip pocket to start the forward swing, then you will make the plane of the swing too horizontal (flat). During this discussion Manuel asks all of the golf instructors, "Does the right elbow get closer to the right hip during the forward swing?" After much imaginary swinging and thought, the students are certain that the answer is YES! Absolutely, the right elbow gets closer to the right hip during the forward swing in comparison to where it was at the address position.

Manuel's answer is, "No, it doesn't." He will let his answer sink in, and the puzzled-looks will begin to grow. He tells the clinic participants to look at him. At the address position the right elbow is a certain distance away from the right hip. Then he will slowly turn his hips to the left, as they will move in response to the forward swing. "See, the body gets closer to the right elbow; it is not the right elbow that gets closer to the body," he says. The right elbow is in about the same place at impact as it was at address. The right hip and the body are in quite a different position at impact than at address. So, it is NOT the right elbow that moves closer to the right hip during the forward swing; it is the right hip that moves closer to the elbow.

· ·

51. WHEN YOU ADD KNEE BEND (AT ADDRESS), THE BODY MOVES AWAY FROM THE BALL IN ORDER TO REGAIN BALANCE.

If the player is in a comfortable address position and he or she adds knee bend beyond their normal, there will be a reaction in the body. The upper torso will change to a more vertical position in reaction to the additional flex in the knees. "When you add knee bend (at address), the body moves away from the ball in order to regain balance," said Manuel.

Manuel is a great believer in the natural instinct of the body to do the best and most simple thing in reaction to any situation if we just leave it alone. Many golfers want to micromanage every muscle and joint when taking the address position when it should be the very simple act of placing the clubhead behind the golf ball. The body will always seek balance so it is not in danger of falling over. In the case of the player who decides that he must add flex in the knees in order to play golf, then he must realize that this change will bring about other changes that may not be desirable.

52. YOUR SHOULDERS ROTATE AT RIGHT ANGLES TO YOUR SPINE. I ROTATE AROUND MY CENTER, THE MIDPOINT BETWEEN THE SHOULDERS.

Manuel was asked if he rotated around his spine during the swing, and his reply was that he did not rotate around his spine. "Your shoulders rotate at right angles to your spine. I rotate around my center, the midpoint between the shoulders," he said.

Then this question was asked of Manuel, "So [if you rotate around your center], your spine may be closer to the target at the end of the backswing than it was at address."

Manuel replied, "It may be. I don't think about it."

He feels that it would be complicated and not very productive to think about the spine during the golf swing.

53. I DON'T LIKE THE WORD *RELEASE*. IF YOU RELEASE A PRISONER, IT MEANS YOU HELD HIM BACK FOR A WHILE.

There have been many discussions about the golf swing that describe a time when the club is "released" during the forward swing. There have also been discussions of a release during the backswing and descriptions of how various sections of the body are "released" during a golf swing.

Many of these come from analyzing video where the club moves quite a bit from one frame to the next.

Manuel explained that the coil (the angle between the left forearm and the club) is retained during the forward swing due to arm speed. In simple terms, the greater the arm speed, the longer the coil or angle will be retained. However, Manuel wanted it to be clear that this "retaining of the angle" was not because the golfer was making an effort to hold the club back. The swinging motion itself will time the so called "release" point of the club. This will be a reaction to the motion that is produced and is not something the golfer should try to produce.

He said, "I don't like the word 'release.' If you release a prisoner, it means you held him back for a while. My club is always free to do whatever it needs to during the swing."

Manuel is always concerned about the different effects that words can have on the golf student. The student could easily interpret "release" to be a suggestion to hold the club back using muscular tension and then to suddenly throw the club into action.

. . . .

54. MY CONCEPT HAS NEVER MISSED A SHOT. I HAVE MISSED PLENTY OF SHOTS.

Manuel always emphasizes the value of positive thinking. He would say that you cannot build anything off the negative things or the problems and that positive thinking could be harder to achieve in our current society because the nightly news is always filled with the negative happenings. Manuel said that his father, Angel de la Torre, a noted golf instructor himself, became known for a particular response he said during a lesson. When the student would miss a shot and ask, "Angel, what did I do wrong?" he would reply, "Why do you want to know? Do you want to do it again?"

So, when you miss shots, you need to return to the concept of what you are to do. It always gets back to that. If a student became stuck in thinking about all of his perceived swing problems, Manuel might ask, "How many ways are there to do it wrong?" There are so many that you cannot list them all, so it is a waste of time to focus your mind on what is wrong. Return to the concept of what you are to do.

"**My concept** has never missed a shot. **I** have missed plenty of them," he said.

. . . .

55. IF YOU HAVE A TOUGH CUSTOMER, YOU SHOULD TRY TO SEE HOW HAPPY YOU CAN MAKE HIM RATHER THAN TRYING NOT TO MAKE HIM ANGRY.

The positive thinking that you need to practice to play good golf can be applied to many situations in life. Manuel said that you can play golf with one of three mental attitudes: 1) **positive** – where you go out and try to produce the swing the way that you were taught, 2) **corrective** – where you are trying to modify your swing to correct for recent errors that you feel that you have made, and 3) **negative** – where you are trying NOT to do things.

Manuel always wants to bring things from the student's everyday life to relate to his golf. He described the golf member who always seemed upset by something that was happening at the golf course and that it would not help the situation by avoiding the individual.

"If you have a tough customer, you should try to see how happy you can make him rather than trying not to make him angry," said Manuel. Clearly Manuel favors mental attitude #1 - the positive attitude, and describes how this can be applied to the golf course or to other areas of everyday life. He related this story that when one of his members returned from a trip and described how difficult the tee shots were on a particular golf course because it had many trees, lakes, bunkers, rough, out of bounds, etc., Manuel asked, "It didn't have any fairways?"

---

56. AFTER YOU HOLE YOUR LAST PUTT ON THE 18TH GREEN, YOU MUST WAIT UNTIL THE NEXT DAY TO HIT YOUR NEXT SHOT.

One student asked Manuel about how to deal with the difficulty created by slow play during tournament golf. Manuel asked the student, "Have you ever played in a tournament of more than 18 holes that lasted more than one day?"

The answer was yes, of course he had played in such a tournament, and then Manuel said, "After you hole your last putt on the 18th green, you must wait until the next day to hit your next shot." This "wait" of many hours between shots did not seem to create any problems for the player, so he was encouraged to adopt a different outlook to any wait between shots during a round of golf.

---

57. IN PUTTING YOUR LEGS CAN STAY MOTIONLESS.

Manuel wants golfers to approach putting differently than the full swing, in that it is the ultimate to have no concern about the club in putting. One need only visualize the ball rolling on the line as far as the hole, and this will trigger the correct actions. On the full swing from the fairway, it is the ultimate to have no ball concern, only focusing on producing the correct motion with the club. In putting, if you visualize the ball rolling on the line you choose, then little else is important.

In building the simplest action for putting, one can use the arms in both the backswing and the forward swing. This differs from Manuel's full swing concept where one must use the hands in the backswing in order to get enough of a coil to produce the speed needed for a full shot. In putting there is very little speed needed to get the job done.

Sometimes a student would "use himself (his body) and carry the putter" rather than swinging it. This movement made it difficult to get the ball started on the line that was selected. Manuel might ask the student to look at the grass between the blade of the putter and the golf ball at address, and to keep looking at that spot and let the putter swing past the spot while rolling the putt. Or he might ask the student to keep facing the ball area with his chest and let the putter swing back and forth, but still have the chest face the ball area even when the stroke is complete. There need be very little body response in the small action that is putting. In fact Manuel went so far as to say, "In putting your legs can stay motionless." He does not mean that you need to tighten the muscles of the legs and lock them down; you simply do not need to use them to roll the putt.

• •

58. WITH 4 OR 5-YEAR-OLD JUNIORS, I WOULD START THEM WITH A 10-FINGER GRIP. WITH 8 TO 10-YEAR-OLD JUNIORS, I WOULD START THEM WITH AN OVERLAPPING GRIP.

Manuel said that he likes the interlocking grip the least because, in people with shorter fingers, it can get the right hand out of position by being too far under the grip. These people make the interlocking of little finger of the right hand and the index finger of the left hand the number one priority rather than the correct positioning of the hands. The key purpose of the grip is to get the hands in position so that, when the club is swung freely and left alone, the club-face will return to a square position when at impact.

The golfer can achieve a good square impact position with either a 10-finger, an overlapping (sometimes called the Vardon grip), or an interlocking grip provided that the hands are in the correct position. Manuel feels that you can change the connection between the hands of the grip as a junior golfer gets bigger and has stronger hands.

"With 4 or 5-year-old juniors, I would start them with a 10-finger grip. With 8 to 10-year-old juniors, I would start them with an overlapping grip," he said.

The position that is important is one where both "V's" (the V's formed by the thumb and index finger of the hands when placed on the club) are pointing to the golfer's center (the midpoint between the shoulders). This is a neutral grip position that should neither close nor open the blade at impact. There are some other specifics of this neutral grip position that are covered in Manuel's book, *Understanding the Golf Swing*.

Manuel has described himself as a "slow grip changer" in his teaching, and he is this way with experienced golfers unless he feels that the grip is the cause of an undesired ball-flight. However, he is insistent that juniors and new golfers learn to grip the club correctly.

∙∙

59. IT'S ALL THE SAME THING. YOU ARE TRYING TO TAKE THE BALL-HITTING ATTITUDE OUT OF THERE.

Manuel had been through several different things on the lesson tee that may have seemed unrelated. For example, he held out a golf club a few yards ahead of the student in the direction of the target and asked the student to try to hit Manuel's club with his swing. The student knew that Manuel's club was just out of the way of the swing, and Manuel cautioned him not to try to "reach" to hit his club, but to simply swing with the intent to hit his club.

Another student was asked to swing the club toward Manuel as he stood about 20 feet ahead of them on the target line. "Swing it toward me," he implored. Still another student was asked to "take the club from the end of the backswing to the finish in ONE movement." They were reminded that the swing was a back and forth movement, not up and down.

In categorizing these different lessons while talking with a group of teaching professionals, Manuel said, "It's all the same thing. You are trying to take the ball-hitting attitude out of there." In one presentation that he was giving to a large group of interested students, Manuel noted all of the teaching professional who were present, and he asked the group of students, "What is the main thing that all of these teachers are trying to do when they give you a golf lesson?" He continued to ask this same question in slightly different ways so everyone listening would have time to give this some thought. "What are these teachers really doing for you? They are making the golf ball disappear," he said.

....

60. WHAT IS ON THE PLANE?

I believe Manuel feels some frustration with the amount of analysis that takes place because of the use of video, especially slow-motion and stop-action video. Not that this video is bad in itself, but it is used to point out the flaws of the student, and it leaves the student with an overload of information with most of it showing negative things.

There are often many lines drawn on the video to analyze the swing plane. Manuel has often pointed out to the teaching professionals how important it is to get the camera on the plane while filming, otherwise you can easily distort the look of the swing. Manuel's book, *Understanding the Golf Swing*, contains a simple definition of the plane: The inclination of the circle the golf club makes when it is swung, with respect to the horizontal level of the ground.

This definition can lead to discussions of the swing plane of an individual as being more vertical or being more horizontal than his normal plane, but if the club is being truly swung, then it will move on a plane. Or, as Manuel writes earlier in his book, "A swinging object never leaves its plane while in motion and its speed is maintained."

During one discussion, where many club parts or body parts may have been related to the swing plane, Manuel asked the question, "What is on the plane?" His answer was, "the swing." This was to get the student's intent back to producing the correct motion rather than trying to find the plane.

61. WRIST ACTION IS ESSENTIAL. HAND ACTION IS TERRIBLE.

It is very important for the student to understand the difference between hand action and wrist action. Hand action is Manuel's term for "using the hands to thrust the clubhead as it approaches the ball," and this he has described as the most common problem in golf. This hand action or thrusting cannot be part of a swinging motion. It falls in the category of casting the clubhead, and it involves the ACTIVE MUSCULAR EFFORT OF THE HANDS TO ADD SPEED TO THE CLUBHEAD.

Wrist action is not to be produced by the golfer; it is "the involuntary reaction of the 'hinges' called wrists to the uncoiling motion of the golf club." Wrist action is not actively created by the golfer, but it is a response to what the club is doing. To help the student understand this difference, Manuel will ask the student to hold his arm out in front of him, and then he will say, "Show me hand action. Move your hand up and down." The student will easily flap his hand to this request. "Now show me wrist action," he will say, and Manuel will ask the student not to use his hand or arm. This request is not so easy to comply with. Eventually Manuel will grab his student's forearm with his hand and he will ask him to relax. Then he will move the forearm up and down in a rapid motion, and the student will see his hand flap quickly about with no effort on his part. "That is wrist action. It is a RESPONSE to the motion," said Manuel.

Manuel often reminds the teaching professionals to be "one step ahead of your students" and, if you were asking them to use their arms on the forward swing rather than using their hands, then watch that they don't get muscularly tight in trying to keep the hands out of the forward swing. Manuel said to one student who was working on this, "No 'hands' [not using the hands on the forward swing] does NOT mean that you freeze the wrists."

In summing up such a discussion, Manuel stated, "Wrist action is essential. Hand action is terrible."

62. WHY DO I REPEAT, OVER AND OVER, WHAT I WANT THEM TO DO?

When Manuel is conducting a teaching seminar for golf professionals, there will be a good bit of time spent with Manuel giving golf lessons to average golfers. The professionals will observe the lessons and then, only after the student has left, Manuel will discuss his procedures and why he did what he did. It is only then that he will answer the other professionals' questions. For Manuel, the student is always "number one." Even in this situation where the student is, in effect, the guinea pig and Manuel is trying to teach his concept to the professionals attending the seminar, Manuel is most concerned that the individual experiencing the lesson will walk away with a better understanding of his golf swing. Manuel wants the student to be very clear and positive about what he needs to do to play better golf.

This also shows how important Manuel feels it is to keep the student on the task at hand. During these teaching seminars, there may be as many as 50 or 60 golf professionals around observing the lesson, and the student may say something that gets a good laugh from the crowd. Manuel may say to the student, "Don't worry about them [the golf professionals]; they are not even here," to get the student's mind back to the interaction between Manuel and the student. And once Manuel gets the student going on the right track, he will keep repeating the same direction. In a discussion with the golf professionals, Manuel once said, "Why do I repeat, over and over, what I want them to do? Is it because they are not smart enough? No! It is because I don't want their minds to wander." He points out that if someone in the seminar commented about the student's swing, then his mind would go right to that, and it would take some time to get him back to the action that he was originally working on.

"What does it take to drive a nail into very hard wood?" Manuel asked this question to have the student realize that it takes more than a couple of good swings to create lasting improvement. He feels that many students do not progress the way they might because after a couple of good swings, they will think that "I have it," and they will go off to do other things rather than continuing to hammer the nail into the hard wood, continuing to practice the swing that they are trying to perfect.

63. THEY TELL YOU TODAY THAT YOUR HANDS SHOULD BE AHEAD OF THE BALL AT IMPACT. THAT, TO ME, IS A RIDICULOUS THING.

Manuel wants golf professionals to understand the difference between a clubface that is "open" and a clubface that is "out of square." An "open" clubface is one where the blade faces to the right (for a right-handed golfer) and the loft is increased. An "out of square" clubface faces to the right and retains its normal loft. This becomes important if the golfer is slicing. If the shot is higher than normal with a slice, then you know that the clubface is "open," and you move to determine the cause of the "open" blade. If the sliced shot is normal height or lower, then you know that the clubface is "out of square," and the cause of this is generally muscular tension in the lead arm during the forward swing. Manuel points out that better golfers tend to play an intentional slice with an "out of square" clubface rather than an "open" one because the shot is of a normal height and does not lose as much distance as when the blade is "open."

Manuel does not like the instruction that tells the golfer to get into impact with their hands ahead of the ball. "First of all they have to figure out how far ahead of the ball their hands should be," said Manuel. And also this tends to produce a slice.

There is one practice drill that Manuel told us would be good for almost any problem: ask the student to swing the club to the end of the backswing and stop; now return the club (the whole club) as it was at address and stop. Now the student is asked to hit the shot with the same intent, without any of the stopping, allowing the club to continue to the finish of the forward swing. So the intent is to simply set the club back to the address position from the end of the backswing and let it continue to the finish. Manuel said that this gives the student a good picture of impact, and it also takes the impulse to "hit" out of the equation.

This drill, while very simple, always takes some time for people to do correctly. In the first part the student will usually use too much effort, and he is forced to try to stop the club back at the address position. Manuel asked one student who was using great strain and effort when all he was asked to do was to return the club from the end of the backswing to the address position and stop, "Would you use that much effort if I asked you to set a glass of orange juice on the table?"

Also, in the first part of the drill, the student may try to move his hips and body the way he would if this were a full swing to the finish. This is not necessary. The student is supposed to simply set the club back to the address position and stop. In the second part of the drill, the student is asked to simply return the club back to the address position and allow the club to continue to the finish without stopping. The body should be allowed to respond appropriately to this full swing.

Manuel has also explained that the legs and body will be in a different position at impact than they would be at address and that the grip end of the club may be slightly higher at impact than at address due to the speed. But he does not feel that it is desirable to have the grip end ahead of the ball at impact.

"They tell you today that your hands should be ahead of the ball at impact. That, to me, is a ridiculous thing," he said.

••

64. NOW, VERY SLOWLY, PUSH MY CLUB BACK.

In Manuel's concept the golfer is asked to swing the clubhead to the end of the backswing using the hands.

This means that both hands should be used equally during the entire backswing. A problem can be seen in the backswing when the grip-end of the club goes out away from the golfer while the clubhead is being flipped inside behind the golfer during the early part of the backswing. When the club is moved this way, it is said to be "laid off." You can say that the club is not being moved in a swinging motion-that the golfer is using leverage, where both ends of the club are going in opposite directions rather than in a swinging motion where everything is moving in the same direction, at the same time, and at the same rate of acceleration.

Manuel describes the cause of the problem as **left-hand dominance** (for a right-handed golfer), or you could call it top-hand dominance. The solution is for the golfer to use the right hand as well as the left during the entire backswing. Some students may improve by starting their backswing correctly, but after a time the right hand gives up and the left-hand dominance occurs, and the club will still get "laid off."

Manuel has many ways to help a student to become aware of and correct this backswing problem. In one of the most effective ways, Manuel, after the golfer had addressed the ball, held a club level to the ground with the grip-end pressed lightly against the back of the student's right hand. The shaft of the club being held by Manuel angled slightly inside the target line in the direction that a correct backswing would go. Then he told the student, "Now, very slowly, push my club back." He explained that, if the student used left-hand dominance, the student's hands would go outside and around the club that he was holding. When the student pushed Manuel's club back as he asked, it forced the hands to move in the correct direction and the left hand could not work around the right hand, using it as a pivot point.

65. DON'T EVER TELL ANYONE THAT THEY DON'T HIT THE BALL FAR ENOUGH.

During a teaching seminar, one of the professionals told Manuel that he was teaching a young girl who had a nice swing and her father told the professional he needed to teach his daughter to drive it 270 yards because she could only hit it 220. Manuel told the instructor to give a lesson to the father and after he hits his drive 230 yards, tell him to hit it 300 yards. Then, after the man hits about 20 or 30 drives, ask him, "Why can't you hit it 300 yards?" "See what he says," Manuel advised. It is hoped that this will get the father to understand that everyone has a potential for distance that they cannot go beyond and to try to do so will only destroy the swing and his or her game.

I have heard Manuel say this to a few aspiring junior players: "Distance will bloom slowly like a flower." In other words, just concern yourself with making a correct swing, and you will get the distance that you should. As Manuel notes in his book, *Understanding the Golf Swing*, "...given a certain size arc, the swinging motion produces the greatest amount of force that can be produced within that arc."

Manuel directed this to all of the professionals in the teaching seminar: "Don't ever tell anyone that they don't hit the ball far enough."

66. IS THE *POSITION* OF THE CLUB TOE-UP AND PARALLEL [to the target line] IMPORTANT? NOT TO ME. THE *MOTION* THAT GETS IT THERE IS IMPORTANT.

During seminars for golf professionals, there is often a great debate about various positions of the club during the swing. In one seminar conducted by Manuel, the question came up regarding a position of the club during the start of the backswing. Should the toe point straight up when the shaft reaches a position where it is level with the ground? Should the toe be on the same angle as the golfer's spine at this point? Should we even worry much about the club at this point?Manuel chose to address the concern for **POSITIONS** of the golf swing. "Is the **position** of the club toe-up and parallel [to the target line] important? Not to me. The **MOTION** that gets it there is important," he said.

Manuel followed-up with one of his many questions: "How many static moments are there in a swing?" He then answered his own question, "Zero!"

Manuel will often ask his students, "What is a swing?" And he will continue the conversation until a student would stop thinking like a "golfer" (meaning "golfer" in a bad sense, as in one who over-analyzes simple things to the point of immobility) and realize that a swing is simply a **MOTION** – a movement. He will encourage the student to this way of thinking by saying, "You are a club-mover, not a ball-hitter." Or, in the case of this professional seminar, you are not a position-achiever.

For the "golfers" (in the bad sense of the word) out there, Manuel was asked about the toe of the clubhead pointing straight up at the first time that the shaft reached a horizontal position in the backswing, and he said that you could have the toe leaning forward, as the golfer's spine, but you would hook the ball if you did not make an adjustment. As for the clubhead at the end of the backswing, if the shaft was level with the ground, the toe should be pointing downward at the same angle as the plane of the particular swing.

• •

67. I DON'T PRACTICE THE DRIVER VERY MUCH.

Manuel always suggests practicing the short game a lot. He will ask, "Why do you need to practice the small shots more than the full swings?" The answer is a simple case of numbers; there are more of them. Your full swing with any club sends the ball a particular distance and then you make adjustments based on the conditions on that particular day, but on a partial swing there is an almost infinite amount of distances and types of shots that you may need to play. While it takes a great deal of practice to be ready for all the possible short game shots, the full shots are mainly about the correct direction.

Manuel told us, "I don't practice the driver very much." He said that if he was warming up to play a competitive round and he hits one driver well on the practice range then, "I will put it (the driver) back in the bag so I don't get corrective or try to overpower the swing." He is always trying to keep the golfer in a positive mental state, focusing on what needs to be done with the swing, rather than moving into a corrective mental state where the golfer begins to change his purpose to try to correct for a perceived problem. He also recognizes that many golfers are more likely to try to add power to the swing when they get the driver in their hands.

• •

68. I DISAGREE WITH USING THE VIDEO TO SHOW PEOPLE WHAT IS WRONG. I DON'T CARE ABOUT WHAT I DO WRONG.

When Manuel was inducted into the World Golf Teachers Hall of Fame in 2005, officials made some cards that were handed out with Manuel's picture and a quote which, appropriately, began with two of his famous questions. It stated, "Do you shop? Do you make a list of all the things you don't want to buy?" This is his plea to the golfer to forget about all of the shots and actions that you are trying to avoid and focus on what you want to do. Manuel wanted golfers to use video of them when they are swinging the correct way, developing a clear picture of the motion, and then put the video away. He worried that if golfers looked at video of themselves too much, then they would begin to find things they don't like about themselves, and the positive focus would be lost. "I disagree with using the video to show people what is wrong. I don't care about what I do wrong," he said.

When discussing the use of video with golf professionals, Manuel asked, "What does the video do?" "It miniaturizes the person." He was not against using video in golf instruction and did use it himself, though it was not a big part of his instruction. But he said that he would prefer to watch the actual person swing rather than a 3-inch image of him on a screen. He also noted the importance of locating the camera in the correct place so one does not get a distorted image. From behind the golf shot you need the camera on the swing plane to get the best information.

· ·

69. IF THE RIGHT HEEL DOESN'T RESPOND [on the forward swing], IT FORCES YOU TO MOVE FROM UP HERE [the shoulders].

Manuel explained that the arms were the initiators of the *movement of the club* on the forward swing, and he wanted the back heel (right heel for a right-handed golfer) to be the initiator of the *body's response* to the forward swing. One student had the club coming from the outside and was getting thin contact on the heel of the clubhead, and Manuel did a slow motion imitation of his swing with the upper body leaning to the left as he moved the club forward. The shoulders were moving in too horizontal a plane. He explained that "if the right heel doesn't respond [on the forward swing], it forces you to move from up here [the shoulders]." In giving the student a sense of the correct response by the right heel, Manuel will often have the student hold a golf ball in his right hand and ask him to toss it underhanded toward the target and allow the right heel to come up with the motion. It feels very awkward to keep the right heel on the ground when tossing a ball underhanded for any great distance.

It seems to go against our instincts but, if your upper body is leaning to the left, and thus the swing center is moving ahead of the ball before impact, then the cause of the problem may be that your back heel, and thus your lower body, is not responding on the forward swing. Manuel told one student, "As soon as your arms start going forward, let the right heel come up."

....

70. IF YOU ARE HITTING A SMALL SHOT TO THE TARGET, YOUR MIND WILL CONTROL THE SIZE AND THE SPEED, BUT YOU CONTROL THE DIRECTION.

Once the fundamentals are in place, Manuel views the process of achieving the correct distance on a shot as an instinctive thing. The instincts are improved by practice, practice and more practice in the short game. And you must visualize the ball rolling as far as the hole just prior to playing a shot to bring these instincts out. Once, when a golfer told Manuel that he was going to work on the speed on a particular putt, Manuel asked him, "How are you going to work on the speed?" You should picture the ball rolling the correct distance, but your conscious mind and your intellect cannot really **work** on the speed of the putt.

Manuel described it this way: "If you are hitting a small shot to the target, your mind [instincts/subconscious] will control the size and the speed, but you [conscious self] control the direction." You select the direction and then, very consciously, aim the clubface and swing to send the ball in that particular direction, but your "feel" for the shot will control the distance.

"All you need when you hit a full shot is direction. The club already has the distance built into it," he said. Manuel has used this same line of thinking to help the student deal with the unnecessary extra effort he may put into a long iron to try to cover the distance. You don't need to add anything to the swing because "the club already has the distance built in it."

....

71. DON'T TRY TO SWING IT TO PARALLEL [to the target line] PAST THE BALL, OR YOU WILL PULL THE SHOT TO THE LEFT.

When Manuel introduces the concept of the swing in a seminar, he explains the geometry of a swing where all of the horizontal cords or lines connecting one part of an arc with another are parallel. For golfers this means that, whenever the shaft reaches a horizontal position during the golf swing, it should be parallel to the target line. These can be good checkpoints and will help give the golfer a picture of the club as it swings. One student asked if he should try to swing the club to the parallel position past the ball area. Manuel responded, "Don't try to swing it to parallel [to the target line] past the ball, or you will pull the shot to the left." Manuel will always ask the golfer to swing the club in the direction of the target on the forward swing. This may seem like a subtle difference, but when the shaft is parallel to the target line, it is pointing to the left of the target. Manuel found that this will give the player a tendency to swing the club to the left and thus pull the shot. So, while the geometric principle is still correct that the club should be parallel to the target line when it becomes horizontal, this should not be the picture for the golfer during the forward swing.

He reminded the golfers that the club does point on the target line for a long time during the forward swing, and it is actually higher off the ground when it becomes horizontal past the ball area than behind the ball. But the purpose for the golfer should be to simply swing the whole club from the end of the backswing to the finish **IN THE DIRECTION OF THE TARGET**.

In discussions on the golf swing, the teaching professionals often get very excited about such minutia and details such as the fact that the club is higher when horizontal past the ball area, and Manuel will say, "Why do you want to know these things? This will not help your students to play better." Manuel told the teachers that such detail was okay for general knowledge, but will not be useful to bring up during a lesson.

••

72. WE SHOULD BE SLOW INSTRUCTORS, BUT EFFECTIVE.

Manuel is like a bulldog during a lesson in that he really stays focused on the student and what he is working on. He keeps the student's mind on the task at hand. He told us that "the golfer's mind is like an explorer, always searching around for something new." The teacher needs to keep getting the student back to what is to be done. He asked the teachers, "If the student does it correctly in the lesson today, what will they be likely to do on the golf course tomorrow?" The answer was that the student would be likely to go back to their original habit for most of the shots on the golf course that next day. The point was that the teacher should not rush ahead to new things just because the student produced some improved swings.

Manuel says that he tries to pick the one best thing which will produce the greatest improvement for any student. "Even though there may be several things that I would like to see improved, I will pick one thing," he said. And he mentioned that sometimes when one area is improved, then some of the other problems may disappear. "We should be slow instructors, but effective," he said.

· ·

73. SWING AT THAT SPOT, AND THE SPOT IS ON THE CIRCLE.

A swinging motion is a circular motion, and as Manuel has asked many students, how many straight lines are there in a circle? When a student uses a pulling action on the forward swing with tension in the lead arm (left arm for a right-handed golfer), this action has what he calls a "straight line attitude." When you are pushing or pulling something, you are applying force in a straight line attitude. When the golfer uses this pulling action on the forward swing, he will hit the shot to the right of the target (for a right-handed golfer).

During one lesson, after the student had worked for a while and was still using that pulling action with tension, Manuel asked him to "swing at that spot, and the spot is on the circle." This spot is a few inches behind the ball, and the spot is on the circle (the correct direction) which is slightly inside the target line. Manuel is very honest with the student and explains that this is a "corrective procedure," and if the student does exactly as he is told, he will begin to hook the shots to the left. If the ball starts hooking, then the student should adjust the spot closer to the ball and then swing for this new spot. In this lesson Manuel felt that he needed a more drastic measure to break the tension that the student was in the habit of using on the forward swing. As soon as possible, the golfer should get to the correct picture, which has the club moving with a tension-free swinging motion from the end of the backswing to the finish, and then the club will move in a circular pattern and not a straight line.

74. WHEN DO YOU FEEL THAT THE SWEET SPOT OF THE CLUBHEAD HAS MET THE BALL?

Manuel asked this question of a golfer who was complaining that his impact was not solid: "When do you feel that the sweet spot of the clubhead has met the ball?" The student and all of the teachers observing the lesson were allowed to chew on this question for a while. (Manuel often told his students that he did not ask these questions to embarrass them or to make them uncomfortable, but to get them to really think.) He then answered his own question this way: "**At address**, when you place the clubhead behind the ball, because when you swing something, it will always return back to where it started." He wants the student to realize that, once the golfer sets the sweet spot behind the ball at address, all he needs to do is to produce the swinging motion and the sweet spot will find the ball without the golfer trying to force it to happen.

Manuel says that you should not work on getting solid contact. If you are not getting solid contact, then you need to find the cause of the problem in the fundamentals or the swing; and when you correct the cause, then you will get the good contact without trying to get it.

75. YOU CAN ONLY HAVE ONE THOUGHT AT A TIME, SO IF YOU THINK OF ALL OF THE DIFFERENT PARTS, THEN YOUR MIND IS JUMPING AROUND-THAT MAKES YOUR MUSCLES JUMP AROUND.

"How often have you heard someone say that I am going over to the driving range to practice my mental game?" asked Manuel. He uses the definition of thought as "a mental direction to accomplish or do something specific." He recommends that you have only one thought for each shot, and if your thought has to do with your backswing, then you should not try to have a second thought on what to do on your forward swing, and vice versa. There is just not enough time to transfer from one thought to the next and expect to get a smooth, repeatable action. It is ideal to have your thought relating to your forward swing rather than the backswing since it is the forward swing that really produces the shot. Manuel points out that if you have the correct motion on the forward swing, then this will cancel out any small problems of alignment or problems in the backswing.

Manuel will differentiate between a thought and an awareness. He defines awareness as "sensing what you are doing at the time you are doing it." You should have one thought for each swing, but you may have one or more awarenesses during the same swing. Your thought could be to swing the whole club from the end of the backswing to the finish, and you could have an awareness that you let your right heel come up in response to the forward swing.

"You can only have one thought at a time, so if you think of all of the different parts, then your mind is jumping around-that makes your muscles jump around," he said. Only being able to have one thought at a time is a general truth for any activity, and trying to have several thoughts in sequence during the 1 – 2 seconds that it takes to produce a golf swing is inviting trouble.

· ·

76. THERE ARE TWO THINGS THAT BEGINNERS WANT TO DO: 1) GET THE BALL UP IN THE AIR AND 2) HIT IT FAR. YOU HAVE TO ELIM-INATE THOSE THINGS.

Some of the most magical moments during the lessons that Manuel will give are with brand new golfers. One of the directions that most every new golfer is given is to "brush the grass." There is also an explanation of the fact that the loft of the clubhead is responsible for causing the ball to get up in the air, and the golfer just needs to get the club to the grass. Manuel wants the golfer to understand that it is not his job to get the ball up in the air.

Further discussion with the new golfer will probably include the fact that he does not need to strain or use great effort to send the ball on its way. His job is to develop a swinging motion with the club, and this motion will propel the ball to the target for him. He is trying to instill the correct mental attitude from the very beginning. "There are two things that beginners want to do: 1) get the ball up in the air and 2) hit it far. You have to eliminate those things," he stressed.

Manuel is also a stickler on understanding the correct grip, address position and alignment for the beginner. Manuel will also continue with gentle reminders during the first lesson. But it is amazing how quickly a good looking motion can begin to develop in the beginner when he gives up the straining to hit the ball high and far and simply brushes the grass.

· ·

77. WITH MUSCULAR TENSION, THE FIRST THING THAT GOES IS DISTANCE. THE SECOND THING THAT GOES IS DIRECTION.

You need arm speed to produce velocity when swinging a golf club, and you need arm speed to throw a ball with velocity. One of the main killers of velocity is muscular tension. If the golfer tries to achieve velocity with the golf club using strain and effort, then this can produce muscular tension. "With muscular tension, the first thing that goes is distance. The second thing that goes is direction," said Manuel. This tension can become a vicious cycle as the golfer loses distance and then strains even harder to get the distance back. This muscular tension may also give the false sense of precision and control, but it produces the opposite. Manuel's common questions at this point are, Do you stiffen your legs if you need to walk faster? Do you stiffen your arm if you need to throw the ball farther?

Manuel was asked how one could achieve velocity with the club without muscular strain, and he said, "It is just like when you throw a baseball." In working with students where tension is the problem, Manuel will often give them an action to perform that requires a tension-free muscular attitude. He would ask them to make a full swing with the purpose of setting the shaft of the club literally on the front shoulder (left shoulder for a right-hander) at the finish of the swing. The club should be level with the ground and parallel to the target line when it comes to a stop, resting on the golfer's front shoulder at the finish. The golfer will often require several swings to begin to achieve this finished position because the muscular tension is still present. Manuel will also explain that the golfer cannot produce a full speed forward swing in this case, because the practice drill is limiting the size of the arc to be used on the forward swing.

Manuel told the teaching professionals that "when muscular tension is the problem with a student, especially with men, it can be a lifetime project." This means that a student with muscular tension as a problem may have to revisit this topic in golf lessons year after year.

78. THE BEST EXPLANATION IS THAT IT IS THE COMPRESSION OF THE SAND AGAINST THE BALL THAT GETS IT OUT OF THE BUNKER.

If Manuel's ball was in a bunker with a higher bunker bank a few yards ahead of his ball, he would visualize the ball going low and burying itself in the bunker bank. This goes along with his teaching on pitch shots around the green where the golfer should visualize the ball going low to promote the correct back and forth motion of the club rather than picturing the ball flying up quickly, which can cause the golfer to use a scooping action with the club. This sudden upward movement of the clubhead will often "blade" or top the ball.

Manuel will explain the bunker shot by telling the student that it is the compression of the sand against the ball that gets the ball out of the bunker. Make a swing in the bunker and scrape the sand and watch where the sand goes; it goes forward onto the green. The golfer should not try to lift the ball or the sand. "The best explanation is that it is the compression of the sand against the ball that gets it out of the bunker," said Manuel. This mental attitude of scraping and using the sand will promote the correct swing as opposed to trying to scoop the ball up and out of the bunker.

There is a special shot that Manuel teaches in the bunker that will really show what the compression of the sand can do. The ball is slightly buried in the sand on the bunker bank, and you can take a middle iron and swing horizontally into the bank and **LET** the club get stuck in the sand. If your clubhead comes upward toward the lip of the bunker then you did not do it correctly. You need to keep the whole club swinging forward and the clubhead will get stuck in the bunker bank. When this force occurs, the sand cannot go straight ahead into the bank; it cannot go downward or sideways into a space that is already occupied with other sand; it can only go upward and forward, and it will take the 1.6 ounce golf ball with it.

· ·

79. WHY DO I SAY *SCRAPE* THE SAND RATHER THAN *HIT* THE SAND?

All of the words used by Manuel during a lesson are carefully chosen. It is difficult to convey motion and action using words, but that is something that the teaching professional is forced to do. As Manuel has said to more than one student, "I don't want you to think about swinging it to the target; I want you to do it. Thought is not action." In playing bunker shots, Manuel will direct the student to **scrape the sand**. In the course of the lesson Manuel may ask the student to restate what he is trying to do, and the student may say, "I am trying to hit the sand." Manuel would correct his choice of words by saying this: "Why do I say **scrape** the sand rather than **hit** the sand?" And he would ask the student to extend his right index finger without holding the golf club. "Now I want you to scrape your left forearm using your right index finger. Now I want you to hit your left forearm," he asks. "Why do I say scrape rather than hit the sand? Because they are different directions," he said. The scraping movement maintains the **forward** action of the swing while the hit is done **downward** at the sand.

On a normal greenside bunker shot, Manuel wants to see a scraping pattern in the sand that comes in shallow, then gets a bit deeper, and then exits the sand gradually. So while the club dips below the surface of the sand, it is still a backward and forward movement and not downward. Manuel has said, "The only time in golf that I want you to swing downward is on a buried bunker shot."

· ·

80. THERE ARE THREE DIFFERENT WAYS TO PLAY A FAIRWAY BUNKER SHOT.

During one clinic Manuel said, "There are three different ways to play a fairway bunker shot." The first way is to swing normal and just plan to "pick" the shot. In the correct full swing, the bottom of the arc is slightly ahead of the ball anyway, so if the arms stay in charge and the intent is to swing forward in the direction of the target, then one should strike the ball before the sand, and no big change is needed.

The second way was to play the shot with a high (player's) center and keep the center up in the same location during the forward swing until impact. The player's center is the midpoint between the shoulders. The golfer is asked to elevate the shoulders slightly at address so that the arms are more extended with no bend in the elbows. You have to be sure that the bottom of the clubhead can still extend to just below the equator of the ball without touching the sand. The additional part to the second option on fairway bunker shots is to keep the player's center (the player's center is different from the center of the swing) up in the same locations during the forward swing. On the forward swing it is normal for the knees to increase their flex in response to the motion. This causes a slight drop in the player's center during the forward swing and is partly responsible for the golfer taking a divot. Since you are trying to minimize the downward movement of the golfer in a fairway bunker, it is helpful to have an awareness of keeping the player's center in the same location during the swing until impact.

The third option is to move the ball back in the stance and still swing forward as if the ball were in the normal position just slightly ahead of the center. This is a good hedge against contacting the sand before impact, because you have moved the ball back where it is located on a higher point of the arc. The tendency on this third option is to make impact lower down on the clubface and to send the ball on a lower trajectory.

81. ON LITTLE SHOTS, I DON'T LIKE THIS IDEA OF ACCELERATING THROUGH THE BALL.

Often the golfer will tell Manuel that he is trying to accelerate through the ball, and Manuel will ask him, "What does it look like when you go through the ball?"

"I have never seen what it looks like to pass through the center of the ball," he says. This is a reminder to the student to clean up his thinking on what he is really trying to do. He might use the phrase that the clubhead passes through the ball-area, but he would prefer you to swing from the end of the backswing to the finish or to swing from one side to the other and eliminate the ball all together.

While discussing a pitch shot near the green, Manuel said, "On little shots, I don't like this idea of accelerating through the ball." He explained that the club will accelerate if you just drop it, and that when people think of accelerating, they begin the forward swing and then add a burst of speed at the ball.

"Would you toss a ball that way?" he asked. And he moved as if to toss a ball underhanded onto the green. The movement began normally and then Manuel added a sudden burst of speed as he neared the point where he would toss the ball.This sudden change of pace can throw off the arc of the swing, can change the alignment of the clubface, and alter the feel for distance.

On the shot where the golfer flubs the pitch shot and the clubhead stops in the ball-area, it is not usually due to a lack of acceleration. Quite often the golfer has added a good burst of speed to the forward swing, but the clubhead slams into the ground, and it is the ground that stops the forward progress.

. . . .

82. I VISUALIZE THE BALL ROLLING ON THE LINE WHILE I MAKE THE (putting) STROKE. I DON'T GET INVOLVED WITH THE MECHANICS.

The fundamentals of a balanced grip, correct alignment, and the address position will be taught in working with beginners on putting, but Manuel wants a different attitude on putting than for the full swing. With putting he wants the golfer to be involved with trying to **ROLL THE BALL ON THE LINE**, and to have no concern for the mechanics of moving the putter. On the full swing he would ask you to be 100% club oriented with no ball concern. This is not to say that Manuel will not deal with the golfer's putting stroke. He does want the golfer to use the principles of a swinging motion in the putting stroke, such as keeping both ends (the butt end of the grip and the putter head) of the putter moving together back and forth. He also recommends that you use the arms in both directions (backswing and forward swing) in putting. This will not apply to the full swing where you will need to use you hands to create the coil of the backswing.

"I visualize the ball rolling on the line while I make the (putting) stroke. I don't get involved with the mechanics," said Manuel. As is always the case with his instruction, all of these words have been carefully chosen and perfected over years of teaching. The golfer should be trying to make the ball roll; you don't hit it, pop it or slap it – you **ROLL** it. Also you see the ball rolling the entire line of the putt; you don't just see the ball at the hole or your "mind may jump" to that part of the putt. You see the ball rolling on the starting line of the putt as well as rolling along as far as the hole. As long as the golfer was able to roll the ball on the line in putting, then that was plenty, and then it just required a lot of practice to develop the "feel" for the correct speed and the ability to read the greens.

83. SOME PEOPLE PUTT IN REVERSE. THEY USE THEIR ARMS GOING BACK AND THEIR HANDS GOING FORWARD.

One flaw in putting technique that Manuel would address is what he called "putting in reverse." "Some people putt in reverse. They use their arms going back and their hands going forward," he said. The modern putting technique is to use the arms to swing the whole putter backward and forward. The hands simply hold the putter, and are not muscularly involved in moving the putter. You can also putt like a mini-version of the full swing where you would swing the clubhead back with the hands and swing the whole club forward to the finish using the arms, but you do not want to use the arms going back and then switch to using the hands on the forward swing.

Manuel told one student to get a small comb or a similar object and place it on the back of the left hand under the golf glove so that it pressed against the wrist and forearm. This stiff object would restrict the ability to use the hands on the forward stroke and give some good feedback if that mistake occurred.

Manuel grew up putting like the players of his day where the putting stroke was like a mini-version of the full swing with the hands used on the backswing and the arms used on the forward swing. He told us that he felt the current players on the professional tours putt better because they have adopted the use of the arms in both directions. Manuel found it easier to change his own putting stroke to the arms back-and-forth technique when he changed his address position. The change was to set up with both arms extended, just hanging down, but without any muscular tension or rigidity. "This eliminated all of the angles [elbows and wrists] and was a big help to me," he said.

84. WHAT SHOULD YOU TRY TO DO ON AN APPROACH SHOT?

"What should you try to do on an approach shot?" asked Manuel. Many students will answer this question by saying that they should try to hit the green. Manuel will respond to that answer this way: "No. That is a result. Never work with results." The golfer should be concerned with producing the motion that will give the result. If you want the ball to go on the green, then select the correct club and make your club swing to the finish in the direction of the green.

Manuel told of observing one of his students who was playing in a professional tour event and was swinging beautifully. Late in the front nine he "went down at the ball on one swing and missed the green." Manuel said that the golfer did not hit many greens after that bad shot.

"Why didn't he hit any greens? He was probably trying to hit the greens," explained Manuel.

. . . .

85. YOUR INTENT NEEDS TO CHANGE FROM HERE [the ball] TO OUT THERE [the target].

Manuel has said that the most common problem he sees in his students is "hand action." This is where the hands are used "to thrust the clubhead as it approaches the ball in order to create more power." The solution is to give your arms the responsibility for the forward swing and to make your focus the target rather than the ball.

"Your intent needs to change from here [the ball] to out there [the target]," Manuel told one student. "You should feel exactly the same as if you were throwing the club down the fairway," continued Manuel. After making some swings that were much better, the student made this observation: "I feel like I'm going to go right over the top of the ball!"

Manuel responded, "Yes, it may feel like the club is never going to reach the ball."

Manuel often reminds the student that any change will give a "contrast of feel" to what was being done as a habit before. He pointed out to the teaching professionals that, if a student has been aiming 25 yards to the right of the target when they are corrected and begin to aim on target, they will feel as if they are aiming 25 yards left of the target.

. . . .

86. YOU HAVE TO WATCH WHEN YOU MAKE A CHANGE WITH A PLAYER.

Manuel usually works with a student just one time at an out-of-town golf school or during a teaching seminar, where he is giving lessons that were being observed by other teaching professionals. At the conclusion of the lesson, Manuel will often have the student restate what he or she was working on so Manuel knows that the student had a clear understanding for future practice. Also, he might find out which teaching professional was working with the particular student and suggest what the next steps could be.

In these teaching seminars Manuel will always wait until the student has moved away before he will answer questions by other teaching professionals about the lesson. When questioned about why he did not work with the student's grip or club position at the end of the backswing, etc., Manuel will explain, "I am not saying that you are wrong; I am just saying that was not my priority. That may be something that we would work on in a future lesson."

"With many players there may be 3 or 4 things that need to be improved, but you must prioritize so that you will work on the one thing that will create the greatest improvement when you are with that student," said Manuel.

"You have to watch when you make a change with a player," said Manuel. "Don't change things when they are playing well; wait until they are not playing as well, and they will handle it better," he added.

87. I WANT TO REMEMBER THE GOOD THINGS BECAUSE I CAN BUILD ON THOSE THINGS. I CAN'T BUILD ON THE BAD THINGS.

Manuel often remarks that students will say nothing and not react at all during the lessons when they are hitting good shots. "It is as quiet as a tomb," he said. But, as soon as they miss a shot, then they become very animated and all of the questions begin. What did I do wrong there? What happened on that shot, etc.?

He explained that during a lesson with Ernest Jones (the renowned golf instructor who wrote *Swing the Clubhead*) or with Angel de la Torre, (Manuel's father) there would be little time spent on dealing with what was done wrong. The student might be told that he simply did not swing the clubhead, and to get his mind back to trying to produce that motion.

"Do you know what I do when I miss a shot? I forget it," said Manuel. He told the student that when you hit a good shot, that is the time to say, what did I do there?

"I want to remember the good things because I can build on the good things. I can't build on the bad things," said Manuel. He felt that the newspapers and television news shows "always emphasized the negative," and we are somewhat conditioned by hearing all of these bad things everyday.

When a student once became fixated on the bad things during a lesson, Manuel asked him, "How many ways are there to miss a shot?" The student soon realized that there is an almost infinite number of ways to miss, so it is only productive to return the focus to what was to be done correctly.

Manuel posed another question, "How many ways are there to hit a good shot? Only one way – to swing the club properly." No matter what the missed shot was, the golfer must get back to what he is trying to do.

78 ~ ○

88. YOU DON'T BEAT THEM WITH YOUR *DISTANCE*. BEAT THEM WITH YOUR *GAME*.

Manuel said that he will not argue against distance as an advantage, but he will argue that distance without direction is useless. He always wants the student to return to the basic principles, and one is that "swinging is the most energy efficient method of producing the force necessary to hurl an object a great distance," as stated in Manuel's book, *Understanding the Golf Swing*. The student must forget about power which can bring about a lot of effort and tension, and those will eventually wreck the very motion that will give the golfer the distance that he wants so badly.

There are so many things, such as the fundamentals of the grip, alignment, proper address, the swing, course management, and the short game that are a part of a good golf game. These need the attention of the golfer rather that the quest for power.

To one tournament player Manuel said, "You don't beat them with your **distance**. Beat them with your **game**."

89. BIG DIVOTS ARE CAUSED BY TWO THINGS: 1) THE DESIRE TO HIT DOWN AND 2) USING THE HANDS ON THE FORWARD SWING.

In discussions about divots Manuel has said that if the swing takes a divot, then that is fine, but the golfer should not try to take a divot. A lot of this has to do with the lie; if the ball is sitting on closely-mown bent grass, then the correct swing may well take a divot. If the ball is sitting on top of higher-cut zoysiagrass, then the correct swing may just brush the grass with no divot.

Manuel has noted that big divots with a downward direction [they start shallow and go sharply downward] are not ideal.

"Big divots are caused by two things: 1) the desire to hit down and 2) using the hands on the forward swing," said Manuel.

In the first case there are many golfers who feel they should hit down on the irons. In fact Manuel mentioned that he felt that many of the tour players of today do try to hit down on the irons with the result being large divots. In his concept, the golfer should swing the whole club forward not downward. A divot that would result from a good swing that was forward would be shallow, horizontal and more symmetrical, (the low point of the divot is in the middle of the divot). Also, the divot should be located on the target-side of the golf ball.

The physics principle at work here is that if one is using an object to send another object in a particular direction, then the direction of both objects should be the same. Why swing down when you want to send the ball forward?

At a lesson with one particular student, Manuel noted that if the divot is narrower than the actual width of the clubhead and it is toe-deep (the toe side of the divot is noticeably deeper that the heel side of the divot) where the toe has undercut the grass, then the club face was "open" as it passed through the ball-area.

The second cause of big divots is when the golfer is making the mistake of casting the clubhead downward at the ball. The arms (not hands) should be used to swing the whole club (not just the clubhead) forward to the finish, in the direction of the target (not the direction of the ball).

90. NOTHING GOES FROM THE TOP [END OF THE BACKSWING] UNTIL THE ARMS SET EVERYTHING IN MOTION.

One cause of a slice is that the golfer uses his or her shoulders to initiate the forward swing. This will cause the club to come from the outside and to cut across the target line. In Manuel's book, *Understanding the Golf Swing*, he outlines 19 causes of slicing in Chapter 5, and using the shoulders to start the forward swing is cause #6.

During one lesson Manuel explained to a student who was using his shoulders to start the forward swing that he was, in effect, delaying the start of the forward swing. His shoulders were being used for a certain time, and eventually the arms would have to be used in order to hit the ball or else he would pass right over the top of the ball. So he was reducing the space he had to really swing the club forward. Add to this the fact that using his shoulders caused the club to approach the ball from the outside, thus producing a slice. It is easy to see why this mistake causes a loss of distance. In this lesson scenario Manuel might ask the student where he should begin to accelerate the club on the forward swing. He will then describe a situation where the student is sitting in a car and he needs to drive it through a wall. "When would you floor the accelerator?" asks Manuel. You should start the club, or floor the gas pedal right away, at the very beginning. You wouldn't go slowly in the car for a while and then floor it right before you got to the wall. You would floor it right away so you could have as much speed as possible when the car got to the wall. Some golfers seem to feel that they should wait until just before impact to apply a burst of speed, but this will not be effective.

In a lesson with another golfer who had a similar problem, Manuel asked the golfer to use his arms from the end of the backswing, not his shoulders. "You are either **USING** your arms or **USING** your shoulders to start the forward swing. You can't do both," said Manuel. This is not to say that the shoulders do not move during the forward swing. They move in response to the use of the arms in swinging the club. Manuel summed it up this way, "Nothing goes from the top [end of the backswing] until the arms set everything in motion."

91. THE ARMS INITIATE THE SWINGING OF THE CLUB. THE FEET INITIATE THE BODY RESPONSE.

Manuel has described how, like a spring being wound up, the body in the golf swing coils from the top down (backswing), and uncoils from the bottom up (forward swing). In Manuel's concept the arms are used to swing the club (the whole club) forward to the finish, and it is this motion of the club that should be foremost in the golfer's mind. The question came to Manuel, "If we uncoil from the bottom up [forward swing], then why doesn't the bottom initiate the motion?"

"The arms initiate the swinging of the club. The feet initiate the body response," replied Manuel. Regarding the feet initiating the body response, Manuel will direct the golfer to "let the right heel come up in response to the forward swing," as it would if you were tossing a ball underhand, or if you were standing and then turned to walk to your left.

92. EITHER YOU ARE BALL-ORIENTED, OR YOU ARE NOT. IT IS JUST THAT SIMPLE.

Manuel was doing a presentation on his concept to a large group of average golfers one night, and he was near the end of the presentation when he asked the group this question: "What am I really trying to do for all of you with these ideas?" He answered his own question this way, "I am trying to make the ball disappear." This definitely got some wheels spinning and some minds working. Manuel explained his answer by saying that he was trying to get all of the golfers to understand and to work with the motion of the club, rather than trying do things to the golf ball. When a golfer is in the hit-the-ball mindset, he often does not know what he does with the club. The golfer becomes so involved with the result of the shot that he has no awareness of what is done with the club.

The student, after missing a shot during a lesson with Manuel, will often ask, what did I do on that shot? Manuel will reply, "You don't know? You are the one who did it."

In an effort to get students to lose their ball-concern, he has asked them, "Right now, can you control that basket of balls [or any other inanimate object in the area]?" After the student acknowledges that he cannot have any control of the object, Manuel will ask him, "Why not? What must there exist between you and the object before you can control it?" **CONTACT!** If you are in contact with the object, then you can control it. "In golf, what are you in contact with?" asks Manuel. The student realizes that he is in contact only with the golf club, and he cannot control the golf ball.

Manuel wants the golfer to strive to be 100% club-concerned on the full swing. During one lesson when the student was attacking the ball rather than trying to perfect the good swing that Manuel had seen him produce, Manuel declared, "Either you are ball-oriented, or you are not. It is just that simple." He outlined a wonderful statement for the golfer to make prior to playing a round of golf: "Little ball, I don't care where you go, but I am going to make my club go on target."

....

93. QUESTION: HOW CAN THE CORRECT USE OF THE ARMS FEEL SO EFFORTLESS? MANUEL: IT IS JUST LIKE THROWING A BALL.

Manuel has often worked with his students on remaining flexible during the swing. Muscular tension in the lead arm during the forward swing is one common cause of slicing. If the student's fundamentals are pretty good, but they get muscularly tight during the swing, Manuel may say, "Your swing is not the problem; you are." In other words, if the student would get rid of the muscular tension, then the swing would work correctly.

The lesson might begin with Manuel explaining that the student needs a lack of muscular tension to produce speed in the golf swing. "Would you stiffen your legs if you needed to walk faster?" asks Manuel. It seems to go against some golfer's thinking that he can move his arms and the club so fast without great strain. The question came to Manuel, "How can the correct use of the arms feel so effortless?"

"It is just like throwing a baseball," was his answer. He has asked the student to swing the golf club up in the air, a few feet over the ground, as if swinging a baseball bat to hit a pitched ball. Once this was done in a normal way, he would ask the student to swing like hitting a baseball again, but to make his lead arm very rigid and filled with muscular tension. "Now how far can you hit the baseball?" he will ask. The student senses the difficulty of producing speed with the presence of muscular tension. The student is often unaware of this tension when he is in his golf mode, but he notices it immediately when swinging the golf club as a baseball bat.

One way that Manuel has used to get the student to remain flexible in the lead arm during the forward swing is to have him swing the club forward and simply set the shaft of the club on the left shoulder. He explains that you cannot use a high speed swing on this practice drill because you are reducing the size of the arc. But the student cannot be muscularly tight in the lead arm and still set the shaft on the left shoulder at the finish of the forward swing. The shaft should be horizontal when it finishes on the shoulder. If the golfer remains tight in the left elbow, then he may finish with the club touching his back, but it will not be horizontal and resting comfortably on the left shoulder. You do want to do this drill with the golf ball so you can begin to feel what it is like to swing forward with a lack of tension in the lead arm.

Another way that Manuel has used to destroy the tension in his students is to stand in front of the student and place his right hand on the grip just below his right hand. He will then try to lift the whole club upward, a few inches off the ground. If the golfer is tight, then his elbows will not give, and his shoulders will go up in the air with the lifting action. When the golfer becomes supple by losing the tension, then the elbows and wrist will give and the shoulders will stay in place. Now Manuel can lift his club and move it anywhere he chooses. In the next step, Manuel will ask the student to set up to the ball and tell him: "I am going to stand in front of you and lift the club and move it just as I have been doing. When I set the clubhead back behind the ball, I want you to go ahead and swing and hit the shot, but I want you to stay just as flexible during the entire swing." When Manuel can feel that the student is flexible, he will set his clubhead back down behind the ball and let go, and back quickly out of the way so he can swing and hit the shot. The student should notice a very different level of muscular tension during the swing if he follows the directions, and this new flexibility will show up in improved shots as he does the practice drill.

94. REMEMBERING THE COLOR OF THE FLAG WILL DO YOU NO GOOD. DO YOU REMEMBER THE *LOCATION* OF THE FLAG?

One student, after a particularly good tournament-round of golf, was talking with Manuel and remarked that he had made a point to really look at the flag before each approach shot, and to even note the color of the flag right before he began the swing. Manuel responded, "Remembering the color of the flag will do you no good. Do you remember the **LOCATION** of the flag?"

In this comment Manuel was quickly directing the student to what was really important. Having an awareness of the color of the flag was not what helped the accuracy of the approach shots; having an awareness of the location of the target during the swing was the important point.

If a student displayed correct fundamentals and a good motion, then Manuel often worked with them on simply "seeing the club going on target" during the swing. During one such discussion, Manuel said that he could still see his club going on target during a round of golf where he won a national senior championship over 20 years earlier. "Your swing is nice, but it is not directed at anything," said Manuel to one student. He did not want the student to try to figure out how to get the club to go on target, but to simply **"SEE"** it going there during the swing.

Manuel told the aspiring teachers during one seminar that he liked to work in various learning styles during the lesson. He will explain a concept and ask questions to see if the student has a clear understanding. This is for the cognitive (auditory) learner. He will put his right hand over the right hand of the student and swing the club with them to give them the **FEEL** of the action for the kinesthetic learner. And, for the visual learner, he will also ask the student to **"SEE"** the correct motion before it is produced and as it is being produced. The student will usually experience all of these learning styles during a lesson with Manuel, so he does not miss his favorite mode of learning.

....

95. MY MENTAL SHOT HAS NO DISTANCE OR ELEVATION.

Manuel does not like yardages printed on sprinkler heads and very detailed hole-location sheets. He feels that we would play as well if we were in the habit of using just our eyes to look at the target and determine which club should be used. In fact, the golfer would do better on a strange course where a convenient yardage marker cannot be found.

"Golf should be a social game, and you see all of the golfers with their noses in their yardage books and pacing off distances," he said. On this same subject Manuel once said, "de la Torre will use yardages when Michael Jordan has to stop the basketball game and measure to the hoop before he shoots!" He also points out that a golfer does not hit the same club the exact same distance from day to day, so one must get a feel for each new shot on each new day.

When Manuel prepares to play a shot he simply looks at the target and gets a sense of what club he should play. If he pictures the shot, then he pictures the ball going in a straight line directly to the target. If this is a full swing then the correct distance is "built into the club," so there is no need to be concerned about the distance. "My mental shot has no distance or elevation," he said. The golfer simply swings the club from the end of the backswing to the finish with no concern for covering any distance or reducing distance. The club also has the desired trajectory built into it, so there is no need to get it up or knock it down. This does not mean that Manuel does not play many different shots. He does, but it is accomplished by changing the ball position or by changing the clubface at address. Once the club and the type of shot have been selected, it gets back to simple swinging the club from the end of the backswing to the finish in the direction of the target. There is no straining for distance or working on trajectory.

In terms of using the yardage to determine the choice of club, Manuel admits that it would take many rounds for the golfer to "train the eye" and the instincts to select the right club, if it has been the golfer's habit to go by the numbers. He feels there would be many benefits for the effort. When asked what Manuel does when he is "in between clubs," he said, "I don't know. It has never happened to me."

He had to smile when recounting the story of playing with one of his assistant professionals in a casual round in Florida during the winter. The young man was unable to find any yardages and asked Manuel, "What club should I use?" Manuel calmly told him to use a 3 wood. In Manuel's world this golfer's trained eye should tell him the correct club, or he should look at the flag and allow his instincts to select the correct size of swing for the club he has selected. But this young man made his full swing and watched as his 3 wood shot was still rising as it sailed over the green only 150 yards away.

Manuel said, "I do yardages backwards." He explained saying that he looks at an object in the distance and says that he would use a 9 iron for the shot, so the yardage is about 125 yards, because that is about how far my full 9 iron goes. He uses the club to tell him the yardage rather than the yardage to select the club.

∙∙∙

96. I DON'T WANT TO MAKE A SLICER HOOK THE BALL.

Manuel does not agree with the idea that a student will need to play worse after taking a golf lesson in order to see improvement in the future. He expects the student to see improved shots during the lesson, and this trend should continue on the golf course during play. When Manuel has a student who has problems slicing his shots, he will try to "cut the slice in half" for a time. Manuel explains to the student that the goal is to turn an average 30-yard slice with the driver into an average 15-yard slice. After a month or so, the 15-yard slice would be cut in half again until, eventually, the drive would be straight.

Manuel has noted that even though a golfer begins to hit it straight during the lesson, it is likely that he will still hit some slices during his next round of golf. If the progress is faster and the slice is eliminated, then that is great, but that is not the normal occurrence.

"I don't want to make a slicer hook the ball," he said. "If the slicer begins to hook the ball, then he will be lost when he goes to the golf course," said Manuel. Where will this slicer aim when standing on the first tee, if he or she has been made to hook the ball for 30 minutes during the lesson? If this change ruins the ability to play on the course, then the student will be less likely to accept the change.

Manuel also recommends that the teacher should not make a change if the student says that he is playing well. One student asked Manuel to look at his putting. Manuel asked him how he had been putting, and he replied that he had been putting well. Manuel immediately stopped that topic for the lesson. He told the student that he did not need to say one more word about putting at this time.

....

97. THE QUICKEST WAY TO WORK ON BAL- ANCE IS TO HOLD THE FINISH.

"Why can't they find a cure for cancer? Because they don't know what causes it," said Manuel. This is said to motivate the golf teachers to work with their students on the cause of the swing problems. While certain flaws in a golfer's swing may appear, it is important to understand the root cause of the flaw. When the cause is corrected, then the flaw will disappear.

It is very noticeable when a golfer loses balance during or at the end of the forward swing. Two common causes for this problem are 1) muscular tension and 2) leverage or hand action during the forward swing.

Manuel explains that flexible muscles and joints (wrists, elbows, shoulders, knees, hips, etc.) are free to respond to all of the speed that is produced on the forward swing. He will demonstrate this by having the student stand upright with his heels on a line; then he will have the student hold a golf club out in front of him, parallel to the ground, with his arms extended. Now Manuel will stand facing the student, and he will take hold of the clubhead. Then he says, "Don't let me push you back over the line." As he holds the student's club and begins to slowly push the club back toward the student, he or she will always stiffen the arms to resist Manuel's pushing. Once the arm and shoulder muscles tighten up, it is very easy to push the student back over the line that the heels were on. Now Manuel has the student try to push him backward while he holds the golf club in front of him. As the student slowly pushes, Manuel allows his elbows to bend and the club to move toward him in response to the pushing. The student cannot push Manuel off-balance without the tension in his arms. He explains that the swing will not throw the golfer off-balance if he or she is flexible and responsive to the swinging motion of the club. If the arms, legs or body become tight and unresponsive, then the speed of the swing can throw the golfer off-balance. You must observe that you are flexible and responsive to the motion you are trying to produce and you will finish in balance.

Another thing that causes the golfer to lose balance is using leverage or hand action rather than using a swinging motion. In a swinging motion everything that is swinging is moving in the same direction, at the same time, and at the same rate of acceleration. Swinging is a great way to produce velocity, like whirling a weight on the end of a string. In leverage one experiences opposing forces. In a see-saw the board is the lever and the bar that the board is attached to is the fulcrum. As one child goes down, the other one goes up. Using leverage is a good way to lift heavy objects, but swinging is a better way to produce velocity.

In Manuel's concept the golfer is told to swing the whole club, from the end of the backswing to the finish, in the direction of the target. When the golfer makes the mistake of using the hands to cast the clubhead on the forward swing, he is using leverage. The left wrist becomes the fulcrum point and the clubhead is cast to the left while the butt end of the club goes in the opposite direction, rather than having both ends of the club moving in the same direction as would occur in a swinging motion. The body often responds to this leverage action by falling off-balance in, generally, the opposite direction of the casting of the clubhead. The leverage or hand action with the cluhead is the cause of the problems; the loss of balance is just one of the symptoms.

Manuel mentioned that he gave a golf lesson to a man who had suffered a stroke. Naturally this student was very fearful of losing his balance and falling. Manuel asked him to hold his finish until the shot hit the ground. "The quickest way to work on balance is to hold the finish," said Manuel.

··

98. I DON'T LOOK AT THE KNUCKLES ON A PLAYER'S GRIP. WHY NOT?

Manuel has called the grip the most neglected fundamental. He recommends that a golfer always take the grip **visually**, that he knows what to look for and check it every time when placing the hands on the club. "You can't go by the feel, because the feel changes from day to day," he said.

He noted that when it is very humid outside, the golfer's hands often feel puffier, and therefore, the grip may feel different. The golfer is urged to ignore the "feel" and put the hands on in the correct position. This "feel" is a subjective thing in the mind of the golfer anyway. Manuel has even given a student the words to say to himself in this situation: "Little hands, you do not feel so good today, but I am going to put you on the club in the correct position and leave you there." Manuel added that, after a few good shots, the grip will begin to feel better to the golfer and the shots will not be spoiled by the grip.

In Manuel's book, *Understanding the Golf Swing*, he describes the grip position this way: "The **V** formed by the thumb and index finger of each hand should point to the center of the body." He also notes, "When the hands are opened [after taking the grip]: a) The palms should face each other. b) The fingers will point vertically downward. With the hands in the position described, they are in balance:

  *With each other
  *With the clubhead
  *With the target line – the direction in which the ball is to be sent.

When the hands are in balance, they do not work against each other, they always complement each other."

Manuel admits that he "is death on grips with juniors and beginners," and he will often not let these beginning students swing until the grip is in the correct position. With experienced players he approaches it very differently and will only change the grip when he feels that "the grip is the cause of the problem" with the ball flight. He explains that experienced players have often built in compensations over the years to accommodate their grip, and changing the grip could bring about a long period of poor shots. This may not be the best route to take to help that player get better.

A "grip check" has been recommended for teachers to use when checking on the student's grip. The student takes the grip and then holds the club out in front of him or her with

Jo Anns

rotary cutter blades

white gingham — small grommetts

elastic cord

hooder clips
broadcloth

Jim Kammer
General Pre-Press Foreman

680 NORTH ROCKY RIVER DRIVE, BEREA, OHIO 44017

216/243-5700

the shaft horizontal. The teacher should stand facing the golfer and hook the two middle fingers of the teacher's left hand (for testing right-handed golfers) over the trailing edge of the clubhead. Now, ask the golfer to let his or her arms be very relaxed, but do not go slack with the grip. Then the teacher exerts a gradual pulling force to stretch the relaxed arms of the golfer. This is similar to the force that the swing should exert on the golfer during the forward swing. If the grip position is neutral, then the clubface will remain square, no matter how much pulling force is exerted by the teacher. If the grip is not in balance with the clubface, then the clubface will twist either open or closed depending where the **V** of the left or right hand is off-center. If either **V** is pointing to the right of the golfer's center, (for a right-handed golfer), then the clubface will twist to a closed position during the grip check. If either **V** is pointing to the left of the golfer's center then the clubface will twist to an open position when the force is exerted during the grip check.

While visually checking the **V's** formed by the thumb and index finger on each hand is the recommended method for taking the grip, Manuel has explained that the **grip check** is the ultimate way to be sure of the correct position for each individual and to convince the player that a grip change is necessary.

"I don't look at the knuckles on a player's grip. Why not?" asked Manuel. He explained to the teachers that depending on the size of the hands, they may look and see a different number of knuckles on the left hand. This is not the ideal method for the golfer to find the correct position for the grip.

··

99. WHEN YOU SQUEEZE THE HANDS, THEY SHOULD NOT CHANGE POSITION.

Manuel will describe the top hand (left hand for a right-handed golfer) as primarily a palm grip, and the bottom hand as more of a finger grip. The grip will be at an angle across the palm of the top hand, and when this hand is closed in the correct position, the **V** formed by the thumb and index finger will point to the center of the golfer.

"The grip is in the fingers of the bottom hand. Why? What is in the palm of the bottom hand?" asks Manuel. He will explain that it is the left thumb that is in the right palm. Some golfers do not readily accept the feel of the grip in the fingers of the bottom hand, and they turn this hand under to get what they feel is a more secure hold on the club. The problem with this is that it causes the **V** on the right hand (for a right-handed golfer) to point well to the right of the golfer's center, and this will cause the clubface to close during the swing.

It can also cause problems if the grip is placed too much in the fingers of either or both hands. The hands may appear to be in the correct position at address (which is with the **V's** formed by the thumb and index finger pointing to the golfer's center), but when more pressure is applied in the fingers during the swing, the hands will change positions. Manuel says that in order to check this position at address, "when you squeeze the hands, they should not change position." If the club is placed too much in the fingers when you squeeze the hands, the **V's** will change position, and this will cause the clubface to be inconsistent at impact. For the top hand the **V** will point to the right of center (closed face grip position), and for the bottom hand the **V** will point to the left of center (open face grip position), if the club has been placed too much in the fingers and the hands are squeezed tightly. If the hands are in the correct position, then the **V's** will point to the golfer's center at address, and even if the golfer squeezes tightly, the **V's** will still point to the golfer's center.

In placing the top hand on the club Manuel says to place the palm against the grip first. "If you start by putting the left thumb on first, then the left hand will end up in a 'weak' position," said Manuel. "Weak" position is a common golf term used to describe when the **V** formed by the thumb and index finger of the left hand (for the right-handed golfer) points to the left of the golfer's center. This position will cause the clubface to become "open" during the swing.

· ·

100. WHY DOES THE HEAD MOVE BACKWARD DURING THE FORWARD SWING?

Manuel repeated the question and then waited for a response: "Why does the head move backward during the forward swing?" Manuel's answer began by explaining that the head is already back at address because the right hand is lower on the club than the left hand, so this makes the right shoulder lower than the left and, therefore, the head is leaning to the right of center (for a right-handed golfer) before the swing even begins.

But why does the head then move back even farther during the forward swing? "Because the right knee is bending so the upper part [body] backs up to maintain balance," said Manuel. In Manuel's concept the arms are used to initiate the forward swinging of the golf club, and the only thing a golfer may need to be aware of about the body response to the swing is that the right heel should come up in response to the forward swing. The right heel comes up in response just as it would if you are tossing a ball underhanded, or you are turning to walk to your left.

Manuel had heard his father, Angel de la Torre, say many times that the body will never make a mistake if it is left alone to respond to the swing. Manuel likes to use everyday examples so that his students "don't think that the game of golf exists in its own universe somewhere." He asked a group of students, "What does your body do when you are driving a car and you make a left turn?" He allowed everyone to make their imaginary left turn in their imaginary car. Then he went on to explain that you lean to the left, but YOU do not think about it. Your mind is on making the turn and turning the wheel of the car, and your body responds perfectly to your intent.

While Manuel can discuss in great detail, and with great sophistication, the many things that occur during the swinging of the golf club, he avoids doing it with students for fear that they will try to manage what should be a very natural response to the action of swinging a golf club. There are some very specific things that the student is asked to do to produce the swing, but he is urged to allow his body to just respond, **IN ITS OWN WAY**, to what he is doing. This is the normal way that people perform everyday activities, and "it should not change just because we spell it G-O-L-F."

101. WHERE IS THE TARGET IN RELATION TO YOU?

Manuel will often stress that the golfer should "see" the club going on target in the forward swing before he begins the swing. There are some students who have developed very nice motions, but Manuel says that their swings "have no direction." He uses the analogy of a very good rifle that is not aimed at anything in particular. It shoots the bullet with great precision, but it will rarely hit the target.

The geometry of the golf swing tells us that shaft of the club should be parallel to the target line each time it reaches a point where it is horizontal to the ground during the golf swing. But Manuel has said that you should not try to swing the club to parallel to the target line past the ball area, or "you will pull the shot to the left." (This refers to the right-handed golfer.) The club should be directed on target, even though it will reach the parallel position slightly past the point when it is on target.

There was one student who was consistently pulling shots to the left, and Manuel asked him, "Where is the target in relation to you?" After some thought and discussion about Manuel's puzzling question came the answer. "The target is to the right in relation to you," said Manuel. The clubhead, the golf ball, and the target all rest on the same line, and the golfer rests inside that line. If the golfer turns 90 degrees toward the target, then he or she will not be facing directly at the target, but the target will be to the right in relation to the golfer. At address the clubface will have the direct relationship to the target, but the golfer will not have this same relationship.

Manuel's question and the subsequent discussion helped this student visualize a slightly different and more correct relationship between himself, the club and the target. Then it was back to making the whole club swing from the end of the backswing to the finish **IN THE DIRECTION OF THE TARGET**.

....

102. THE *DIRECTION* OF THE BACKSWING AND THE FORWARD SWING SHOULD BE THE SAME, BUT THE *PATH* IS DIFFERENT.

"Return the club in the same circular direction that you go back," is a common instruction given by Manuel and can by used to correct several problems with the swing. He told a group of teachers that this was an easy way to work with students who use their shoulders to begin the forward swing rather than using the arms. When the shoulders are used in a horizontal fashion to begin the forward swing, the club will approach the ball from outside of the correct direction (outside in). Manuel said it was easier for the student to work with a small part of the circle directly behind the ball, because he can see it. Even though the problem of using the shoulders may start at the beginning of the forward swing, the student cannot see the club at this point. If he focuses on returning the club in the same circular direction that he used on the backswing, then he will **begin** the forward swing in the correct direction.

In working with a student who was returning the club from the outside, Manuel might take another club and hold it vertically and put the butt end of the grip against the ground, on the target line, about a foot and a half behind the golf ball. He will tell the student, "Don't hit my club." The student will make the backswing, and as the student begins his forward swing, Manuel will slip his club several inches away from the target line so if there is another mistake with the swing, the student will not strike the club he is holding against the ground. Often, after the first swing with this drill, the student will say, "I was afraid. I didn't want to hit your club!" Manuel will respond, "Good."

Another way to achieve this is to tee up one or more golf balls just outside the correct direction for the golf swing and a few inches behind the ball to be struck. If the student started back outside the correct direction, or he returned the club outside the correct direction, then he will hit these other balls. "Do you know what some of my members call this drill? The Spanish Inquisition," Manuel has said with a smile.

If needed, Manuel will explain, "The **DIRECTION** of the backswing and the forward swing should be the same, but the **PATH** is different." The direction is defined in Manuel's book as "the line or course on which something [golf club] is moving or is intended to move." The path is defined as "the arc described by the clubhead. The path of the forward swing is not the same as the path of the backswing."

Manuel asked one student to draw lines in the sand to

describe his picture of the arc of the backswing and the arc of the forward swing. When the student drew the arc of the backswing and then retraced it to represent the arc of the forward swing, Manuel explained that this was not correct. The arc of the forward swing is closer to the target than the arc of the backswing, and that you would need to make the mistake of casting the clubhead to try to make the two arcs match up. So while it is ideal to make the **direction** of the backswing and the forward swing the same, the **arc** that the clubhead travels on should be different.

....

103. THE LANDING SPOT PICKS THE CLUB FOR YOU, BUT YOU SEE THE BALL ROLLING AS FAR AS THE HOLE.

Manuel was asked if he focused on the spot on the green that the ball was to land when playing pitch shots around the green. "No. The landing spot picks the club for you, but you see the ball rolling as far as the hole," he replied. He added that if you focused on the landing spot, you would tend to come up short of the hole on the pitch shots. One of the few times he suggested focusing on the landing spot was when the ball would have to land short of the green in order to have it end up at the ultimate hole location.

Manuel explained his process saying that he looked at the shot and picked the spot where he wanted to land the ball, and then he "went back to my bag and looked at my clubs and said to them, 'Which one of you guys can produce this shot for me?' " But once the club was selected, the projected landing spot was set aside, and the focus was back to the golf hole and seeing the ball rolling as far as the hole.

What is needed to train our instincts to have the "feel" for the correct distance on these little shots is "practice – practice – practice," said Manuel. He also said that, when the golfer focused on the hole and played a successful pitch shot, the ball often landed on a different spot than was originally selected. The golfer's trained instincts were used to "feel" the correct distance for the shot, and the intellect was used only in the strategy and planning stage.

....

104. NO. I TEACH ABOUT MOTION.

In December of 2006, Manuel de la Torre was inducted into the PGA Golf Professional Hall of Fame with, among others, Jack Nicklaus. The ceremony was held in conjunction with the PGA of America's Teaching and Coaching Summit, and Manuel was on the agenda doing a golf lesson with one of his notable students, Tommy Aaron, the 1973 Masters Champion. During this lesson Manuel worked with Tommy on swinging the whole club from one side to the other with no concern for going at the golf ball. This lesson was in contrast to some of the other presentations which contained a lot of detailed information and video examples of various angles and positions that the golfer was supposed to achieve.

After doing his lesson for the Teaching Summit participants to observe, Manuel walked off the tee and was interviewed by a writer doing an article about the Teaching and Coaching Summit. The writer asked Manuel, "Do you always teach about feel, like the lesson with Tommy Aaron?"

"No. I teach about motion," replied Manuel.

When a student says that he wants to have the feel of the swing, Manuel has asked him, "What comes first, the action or the feel?" This question is intended to get the student to realize that he must begin by having a clear picture of the motion that he is to produce with the golf club, and then he simply produces it. Once the action has begun, the golfer can sense what is happening, and this is the "feel." The golfer should not set out to reproduce the feel of a particular swing; he or she should try to produce the correct motion with the club, and the feel will follow.

Manuel asked a group of students, once they had hit their tee shot off the first tee, if they had ever played that same exact shot at some time in the past? Have they ever had that exact lie, distance, temperature, wind, hole location, firmness of the green, feeling the way they feel on that day, etc. before? Obviously the answer is no. So how can you reproduce the feel of a shot that you have never faced before?Set out to do the right thing with the golf club, and while the shot may make you feel good, it is unlikely that any shot in the future will feel exactly the same as the one you just played.

....

105. THE UPPER BODY IS STACKED OVER THE LOWER BODY. HAVE YOU EVER SEEN THIS IN REVERSE?

For several years Manuel has conducted a three-day seminar for teachers in Phoenix, Arizona. He will often begin the seminar by reading some golf instruction articles that have appeared in the popular golf magazines in the past year. One such article described the problem of "skying" the driver, where the ball strikes the top of the clubhead, just above the clubface, and goes very high and short. The article attributed the problem to an open clubface.

He pointed out that the type of shot that is described in the article, where the golf ball leaves a mark on the top of the driver clubhead, can only be hit with a closed clubface. If you hold the clubhead of a driver next to the golf ball and then open the clubface, you will see that the top of the clubhead cannot strike the golf ball. Now close the clubface, and you will see that the top of the clubhead can strike the ball, especially if the clubhead is going downward.

"Has the author of this article ever tried this for himself?" said Manuel. This is Manuel's plea for better articles about the golf swing so that "golfers don't become confused and lose respect for teachers." He encourages all teachers to try all of these shots for themselves so they understand them and can demonstrate the shot for their students. He assured the golf professionals that this will not hurt their own golf games and will make them better, because they will truly understand the cause and effect of problem shots.

Manuel described how he and his father tried to figure out how a certain wedge shot was hit, so Angel went out in front of the green with a sheet of paper and would record what he was trying as he hit shots into the green. Manuel would be at the green and he would record the reaction of the golf ball on every shot. Then they would switch places with Manuel trying the shots and his father recording the reactions of the golf ball. Then they would compare the notes. In this case, the wedge shot was one where the ball came in lower, took a big skip and then stopped quickly. After many such practice sessions they determined that the shot could be hit when you "swung it (club) more forward." Manuel recommends that teachers try out things themselves before using them in lessons.

The need to choose exactly the right words to describe the golf swing is why it took Manuel so long to write his book, *Understanding the Golf Swing*. He does not want to use any words that can be misinterpreted or put forth any concepts that can be overdone by the student.

Manuel read this line from another article which set out to describe the address position: "The upper body should be stacked over the lower body." He then looked up from the paper and asked, "Have you ever seen this in reverse?"

106. THE GAME OF GOLF WILL BE A LOT MORE FUN IF YOU JUST REMEMBER YOU ARE HUMAN AND YOU ARE GOING TO MAKE MISTAKES.

"Swinging the club from one side to the other and hitting a good shot is easy to do. Anyone can do it. But the game of golf is difficult. Why?" asks Manuel. He explains that in most sports the participants get to make a few mistakes, and it does not cost them. You can miss the ball twice and then hit a home run in baseball. In tennis you get to miss your first serve and you get another chance. "But in golf you have to go play your foul balls," said Manuel.

"What do I do when I miss a shot? I forget it," he said. The golfer is urged to get his or her mind back on what is to be done. That is the only thing that matters.

"The moment people miss a shot they think the swing is falling apart, and it is just not the case. You don't want to get corrective," said Manuel. The student is never allowed to dwell on mistakes or missed shots during a lesson with Manuel. The student will make no progress by trying to avoid potential problems or by trying to correct mistakes that occurred in the past. The mind should be used to form a picture of what is to be done with the golf club on **THIS** swing.

"The game of golf will be a lot more fun if you just remember you are human and you are going to make mistakes," counsels Manuel. During a lesson with Manuel, the student soon realizes that he can produce the golf swing. It is not some secret move known only to a select few. And, when the student leaves the mental interferences behind and produces the perfect swing and the shot comes off just as planned, Manuel advises that he say to himself, "Look what a great shot my club hit for me."

GOLF. The result of swinging the club over the shoulder with

Glossary of Terms

Reprinted from Manuel de la Torre's book, *Understanding the Golf Swing*, courtesy of Warde Publishers, Inc. To get a copy of Manuel's book or his DVD call (800) 699-2733 or go online at www.wardepub.com.

ACCELERATION A constant increase of speed per unit of time or space.

ARM The section of the upper extremity from the shoulder to the elbow.

AWARENESS Sensing what you are doing at the time you are doing it.

CENTER

For the player: The midpoint between the shoulders.

Of the stance: The point where a perpendicular line from the center for the player meets the ground.

CENTRIFUGAL FORCE The force created when the golf club is swung. It is an outward pull from the center.

CHANGE OF PACE An effort exerted by the player to increase speed as the clubhead reaches the ball.

CLUBFACE CLOSED Clubface faces to the left (right for left handed players) but the loft is decreased.

CLUBFACE OPEN Clubface faces to the right (left for left handed players) but the loft is increased.

CLUBFACE OUT OF SQUARE Clubface faces to the right or left but retains its normal loft.

COIL The result of swinging the club over the shoulder with the hands in the backswing with the wrists extremely free. If wrists are firm, there can be no coil.

CONCENTRATION Sustained thought over a certain period of time.

CONSTANT Something invariable or unchanging.

DIFFERENTIAL RELAXATION Every part of the body, arms, forearms, and wrists remain flexible, except the fingers that are holding the golf club.

DIRECTION The line or course on which something (golf club) is moving or is intended to move.

FEEL To sense what is being done. Feel cannot be reproduced, it depends on an action that comes first. Feel also refers to sensing the distance when less than full shots are used such as in the short game.

FLEXIBILITY Lack of muscle tension.

FOLLOW-THROUGH The name given to the part of the swing from the ball to wherever the swing ends. The follow-through is produced by the speed of the swing, it is not produced by the player.

GRIP PRESSURE Holding the club with sufficient force to control the length of the club and the speed with which you want to swing it. The pressure should be constant from the player's standpoint throughout the golf swing.

HAND ACTION Using the hands to thrust the clubhead as it approaches the ball in order to create more power.

HIT, A A sudden exertion of effort to send the ball on its way.

INTERFERENCE Anything that changes the initial intent of the player after the swing has been started.

LEAVE IT ALONE Once the forward swing has been started, there should be no additions or subtractions. Examples of additions are trying to increase speed as the ball is approached or trying to give the shot great height through swing changes. An example of subtraction is decreasing the swing speed, thinking that too big a swing has been made and the ball is going to go too far.

LEFT-HAND DOMINANCE Using the left hand exclusively in the backswing. It causes the plane to become flatter (more horizontal – laid off.) Both hands should be used equally.

LEVERAGE Action which consists of opposite forces.

LIE How the ball rests on the ground.

LIES, TYPES OF
  Sidehill Lies – are those where the hill rises or descends to
  the right or to the left of the player facing the ball. One foot
  is always higher than the other.

  Uphill Lies – are those where the hill rises in front of the
  player. The ball is above the player's feet.

  Downhill Lies – are those where the hill descends in front of
  the player. The ball is below the player's feet.

MENTAL DIRECTION The mind telling the muscles what to do.

MENTAL DIRECTION, DETERIORATION OF Taking
  good results for granted. Becoming mentally lax, losing
  focus on what has to be done, expecting the good results to
  just happen, as though the player is not involved.

OBSERVATION Being aware of what is going on. Being
  aware that what should be done is being done. This is positive observation.

PATH The arc described by the clubhead. The path of the forward swing is not the same as the path of the backswing.

POINT OF MAXIMUM SPEED The point where the club
  swings the fastest. The acceleration must be maintained to
  this point, which is the midpoint of the arc.

PRACTICE Just hitting balls is not practice. Practice should
  be performed with a goal in mind.

RADIUS A line extending from the center to the curve.

RESPONSE The activity of the body resulting from the golf
  swing.

RHYTHM The relationship of one side of the swing to the
  other.

SPEED The result of acceleration.

SWING A to and fro motion – backward and forward.

SYNCHRONIZATION The result of synchronizing, which means to make motions exactly simultaneously. To have actions take place at the same time.

TARGET The destination – what we want to reach.

TEMPO The rate or speed of motion.

THOUGHT A mental direction to accomplish or do something specific.

TIMING All parts of the club reach the moment of truth at the same time.

TRAJECTORY, LAWS OF The farther an object is propelled, the higher it is sent. The shorter the distance, the lower it is sent.

TRUTH, MOMENT OF When the clubface meets the golf ball.

VISUALIZATION Forming a mental image of what you are trying to do.

WRIST ACTION The involuntary reaction of the hinges called "wrists" to the uncoiling motion of the golf club.

Quiz on Manuel's Glossary of Terms

1. Clubface faces to the left (right for a left-handed golfer) but the loft is decreased:

   _____

2. Something invariable or unchanging:

   _____

3. Differential relaxation:

   _____

4. Using the hands to thrust the clubhead as it approaches the ball in order to create more power:

   _____

5. An action which consists of opposite forces:

   _____

6. Flexibility:

   _____

7. Left-hand dominance:

   _____

8. Arm:

   _____

9. What describes correct grip pressure:

   _____

10. Acceleration:

    _____

11. Speed:

    _____

12. Tempo:

_____

13. Rhythm:

_____

14. The involuntary reaction of the hinges called wrists to the uncoiling motion of the golf club:

_____

15. Swing:

_____

16. The force created when the golf club is swung. It is an outward pull from the center:

_____

17. All parts of the club reach the moment of truth at the same time:

_____

18. The moment of truth:

_____

19. Plane:

_____

20. Path:

_____

21. The line or course on which something (the golf club) is moving or is intended to move:

_____

22. Radius:

_____

23. CENTER, for the player:

_____

24. CENTER, of the stance:

_____

25. The name given to that part of the swing from the ball to wherever the swing ends. It is produced by the speed of the swing; it is NOT produced by the player:

_____

26. Forming a mental image of what you are trying to do:

_____

27. The mind telling the muscles what to do:

_____

28. Awareness:

_____

29. A mental direction to accomplish or do something specific:

_____

30. Concentration:

_____

31. Feel refers to sensing what is being done. Feel cannot be reproduced; it depends on an action that comes first. What is the other use of the term "feel":

_____

32. Being aware of what is going on. Being aware that what should be done is being done. This is positive

_____.

33. The result of swinging the club over the shoulder with the hands in the backswing with the wrists extremely free. If the wrists are firm, this cannot happen:

_____

34. Clubface out of square:

_____

35. Is it ideal for the PATH of the forward swing to be the same as the path of the backswing? (Yes or No) _____

36. Is it ideal for the DIRECTION of the forward swing to be the same as the direction of the backswing? (Yes or No)

_____

37. A sudden exertion of effort to send the ball on its way:

_____

38. Anything that changes the initial intent of the player after the swing has been started:

_____

39. Where is the point of maximum speed:

_____

40. Taking good results for granted. Becoming mentally lax, losing focus on what has to be done, expecting good results to just happen as though the player is not involved:

_____

41. To make motions exactly simultaneously. To have actions take place at the same time:

_____

42. Laws of trajectory:

_____

43. The destination – what we want to reach:

_____

44. Just hitting balls is NOT _____. _____ should be performed with a goal in mind. (The same word for both blanks.)

Quiz on Manuel's Glossary of Terms Answer Key

1. Clubface closed
2. Constant
3. Every part of the body, arms, forearms, and wrists remain relaxed, except the FINGERS that are holding the golf club.
4. Hand action (an error)
5. Leverage
6. Lack of muscle tension
7. Using the left hand exclusively in the backswing. It causes the plane to become flatter (more horizontal – laid off). Both hands should be used equally.
8. The section of the upper extremity from the shoulder to the elbow.
9. Holding the club with sufficient force to control the LENGTH of the club, and the SPEED you wish to swing it. The pressure should be CONSTANT from the PLAYER'S STANDPOINT throughout the golf swing.
10. A constant increase of speed per unit of time or space.
11. The result of acceleration.
12. The rate or speed of motion.
13. The relationship of one side of the swing to the other.
14. Wrist action (a correct response)
15. A to-and-fro motion, backward and forward
16. Centrifugal force
17. Timing
18. When the clubface meets the golf ball.
19. The inclination of the circle the golf club makes when it is swung, with respect to the horizontal level of the ground.
20. The ARC DESCRIBED by the clubhead. The path of the forward swing is NOT the same as the path of the backswing.
21. Direction

22. A line extending from the center to the curve.
23. The midpoint between the shoulders
24. The point where a perpendicular line from the center for the player meets the ground.
25. Follow-through
26. Visualization
27. Mental direction
28. Sensing what you are doing at the time you are doing it.
29. Thought
30. Sustained thought over a certain period of time.
31. Feel also refers to SENSING DISTANCE when less that full shots are used such as in the SHORT GAME.
32. Observation
33. Coil
34. Clubface faces to the right or left but retains its normal loft.
35. No
36. Yes
37. A hit
38. Interference
39. The midpoint of the arc
40. Deterioration of mental direction
41. Synchronization
42. The FARTHER an object is propelled, the HIGHER it is sent. The SHORTER the distance, the LOWER it is sent.
43. Target
44. Practice

Ordering Information

For information on ordering *Learning Golf with Manuel* go to our website: learninggolfwithmanuel.com or send an email to: book@learninggolfwithmanuel.com.

The price per book is $18 plus $4.00 for shipping and handling. Add $1.00 for shipping for each additional book ordered. If you order 10 books or more the price per book is $11.50 and the freight is free! If you order 30 or more books the price per book is $8.21 and the freight is free. Add 7% sales tax for all books ordered in the state of Missouri. Please copy the order form on the next page and use it to order *Learning Golf with Manuel.*

For information on the book or teaching programs offered by John Hayes, PGA Golf Professional, you can send an email to: jh@learninggolfwithmanuel.com or write to: John Hayes, 523 Fairways Circle, St. Louis, MO 63141

(Order form on next page)

Order Form

Quantity	Item	Total
_____	*Learning Golf with Manuel* book(s) - $18.00 per	_____
_____	10 or more copies of the book - $11.50 per	_____
_____	30 or more copies of the book - $8.21 per	_____

Shipping and handling for 1 copy - $4.00 + $1.00 for
each additional copy ordered (e.g. 3 books = $6.00)   _____

Shipping and handling for sales of 10 books or more -   FREE

7% Sales Tax Missouri sales only   _____

GRAND TOTAL - _____

Your mailing address: _____

_____

_____

Please make <u>check</u> payable to: **Hayes Golf Pro Publishing**
                              523 Fairways Circle
                              St. Louis, MO 63141
                              OR
<u>Mastercard or Visa</u>: name on card:_____

Card #: _____   Exp.: _____

PIN #: _____   Signature: _____